HE IMPACT EFFECT

TOMMY**SPARGER**

THE
IMP**ACT**
EFFECT

A REVOLUTIONARY **VISION**
FOR **COMPASSION**
IN YOUR **COMMUNITY**
AND THE **WORLD**

 Influence

www.InfluenceResources.com

Published by Influence Resources
1445 N. Boonville Ave., Springfield, Missouri 65802

Published in association with The Quadrivium Group—Orlando, FL
info@TheQuadriviumGroup.com
and New Vantage Partners—Franklin, TN
info@NewVantagePartners.net

Cover and interior design by Allen Creative—Snellville, GA
Cover photo of Tommy Sparger by Kaci Moore—Springfield, MO
Typesetting by Wellspring Design and Jay Victor—Nashville, TN

ISBN: 978-1-936699-07-0

First printing 2011

Printed in United States of America

TABLE OF **CONTENTS**

ACKNOWLEDGEMENTS

Thank you Kirk Noonan for your partnership and help.

Thank you Hal Donaldson for believing in this project from the very beginning.

Thank you Greg Marquart, and Adam and Jamie Swenka for leading, innovating, implementing, and directing ImpACT at North Point Church. You made the ImpACT vision a reality.

Thank you North Point Church for giving of your resources and time to ImpACT. You have made your community and world a better place. I am in awe of you and, needless to say, very proud.

Thank you Angie McDonald for all of your hard work.

IMPERILED TERMINOLOGY

In the desperately impoverished country of Haiti on January 12, 2010, one of the most horrific earthquakes in modern history annihilated 225,000 people. I toured the devastated region with Hal Donaldson, president and founder of Convoy of Hope, and upon our return, he visited my church. As we explained what we had seen in Haiti, someone asked Hal, "Where was God during the earthquake?"

Hal paused and then responded simply, "No matter what the tragedy, the question isn't 'Where is *God*?' The question is 'Where are *you*?'"

Tragedies strike every day throughout the world. Some are sudden and shocking, like the earthquake in Haiti. Others creep into people's lives, slowly consuming them. Hunger, poverty, and illiteracy are tragedies like that. Either way, the heartbreaking situations show the victims no mercy.

The difference between the results of each kind of calamity often lies in the reaction of those not directly affected. Swift, sudden destruction usually elicits a quick, compassionate response. But the slow, grinding misery of poverty causes blame-the-victim and turn-the-back reactions just as often as it does mercy and comfort. And these negative responses to the slow-burn tragedies frequently come from surprising places.

Code Words?

"I beg you, look for the words 'social justice' or 'economic justice' on your church Web site. If you find it, run as fast as you can. Social justice and economic justice—they are code words. Now, am I advising people to leave their church? Yes!" [1]—*Glenn Beck on Fox News*

---

1.   Glenn Beck, in a sound byte from his radio program, March 2, 2010.

That means you might be tempted to leave a church whose Web site says something like this:

> ImpACT is North Point Church's outreach strategy to attack the four global giants of disease, poverty, illiteracy and spiritual emptiness. To attack these giants, we partner with local *social justice* organizations.

That means you might want to leave a church like *mine*. But I hope you wouldn't, even though that quote comes from my church's Web site.

If the critics of social justice are right, church leaders like me are waist deep—or more—in trouble. I've promoted social justice for years at my church in Springfield, Missouri. It's a mainstay of our missions outreach strategy.

To be fair to folks like Glenn, I agree that the words "social justice" have been co-opted—and thereby corrupted—by some who lean in directions I, too, find objectionable. It conjures up fears of government programs running amuck. Used in this way, "social justice" smacks of socialism. But when I encourage social justice, I'm not advocating un-American political interference in the lives of my countrymen. I'm simply admonishing people to live like Jesus did.

As I see it, "social justice" is a term that refers to a proper, God-honoring response to the relentless tragedies of poverty, hunger, and illiteracy. And Glenn Beck would probably agree that churches should be at the forefront of addressing problems like these.

We should all be willing to make sacrifices, give of our finances, and shoulder a share of the responsibility to help the poor and suffering. I don't advocate equality through a political system which demands the redistribution of power, wealth, and land. Nor am I pushing any philosophies that Mao, Hitler, or Stalin would approve of. When I say social justice, they're "code words" for the compassion of Christ.

My guess is that you're a loyal American, and, like me, you believe in democracy, free markets, freedom of speech, the press, and the package of rights we hold to be "self-evident."

You respect the intentions of our Founding Fathers and take seriously the God-ordained endowments referenced in the Declaration of Independence.

But deep in your soul, you feel that somehow your own "pursuit of happiness" is tied up with the well-being of other people. You feel called to do more for this world than just maintain a self-satisfied kingdom within the walls of your home and church. Instead, you want to help those who are in need—whether a homeless woman in your city or a hungry kid on the plains of Africa. Perhaps this scripture from James resonates with you:

> What good is it, my brothers, if a man claims to have faith but has no deeds? Can such faith save him? Suppose a brother or sister is without clothes and daily food. If one of you says to him, "Go, I wish you well; keep warm and well fed," but does nothing about his physical needs, what good is it? (James 2:14-16)

2,000 Years of Compassion

If that scripture moves you, the concern you feel is directly from God. It's scriptural. It's right. Don't feel bad because you care about those who are struggling. I encourage you to let the words of Jesus inspire you to do everything you can to transform people's lives in your church, community, and the world. Don't let sound bites from a political pundit or talk show host direct your actions.

Biblical social justice is simply the Church—your church!—having a heart for the poor and suffering and doing something about it. Step back 20 centuries, and consider Jesus entering the synagogue in Nazareth one Sabbath. He picks up a scroll and reads these momentous words from the prophet Isaiah:

> The Spirit of the Sovereign Lord is on me, because the Lord has anointed me to preach good news to the poor. He has sent me to bind up the brokenhearted, to proclaim freedom for the captives and release from darkness for the prisoners. (Luke 4:18-19)

Jesus still calls His Church to be as revolutionary as He was. He wants His followers to meet the full range of physical and spiritual needs that press upon the inhabitants of this fallen world. He wants church leaders to implore, encourage, and make ways for their people to serve the hurting and impoverished. In short, He wants the Church to help connect people's compassion with opportunities to serve.

I know that can be easier said than done. I've served in many churches and have endured an array of attitudes when it comes to the poor and suffering. But I never knew how it would transform a church to wholeheartedly embrace those in need until we launched ImpACT at North Point Church just a few years ago.

Since then, I've seen skeptics of Christianity, the Church, and of Jesus Himself change their minds about all they ever doubted. When a church is bent on serving the poor and suffering to the point that it will "put its money where its mouth is" something dramatic changes in the way people perceive the Church, its mission, and the people it touches.

More than likely, your church is filled with good people. Some may want to make a difference but don't know how, and others might need only a nudge or two to open their eyes to the needs around them. You can show both kinds of people how to live outside themselves by embracing social justice.

In these pages, you'll find the inspiration, tools, and know-how to reach into your community, partner with social justice organizations (to avoid duplication of effort!), and transform people's lives for Jesus. Take on the challenge, and I believe your church will become healthier, stronger, and *bigger*. You'll also see people in your community turn to your church in times of need. And perhaps most importantly, you'll see people around you living like Jesus did.

Each of the ImpACT strategies in this book is designed to get you thinking about how you and your church can make a difference in the lives of people in your church's purview. It may take only one or two new ideas to fuel your creative resolve, jumpstart stimulating conversations with your staff, or simply get you thinking about specific ways your church can make a difference in your community. Consider this book a guide on how you can reach your community in revolutionary ways for Jesus. You might have to tweak a strategy or two to achieve your goals, but commit to changing your community and church, and you will.

The way you ultimately do ImpACT will be determined by you, your people, and the needs represented in your community. The journey is yours to take. What might work in Bakersfield won't work in Philadelphia. But have at it. It's time for your church to transform lives locally that will make a difference globally. And be changed itself in the process.

CHAPTER 1
AN IMPLORING QUESTION

What is your responsibility to the poor and suffering?
People in the Bible often answered questions about responsibility with questions of their own. Questions like:

- Am I my brother's keeper? (Genesis 4:9)
- Who is my neighbor? (Luke 10:29)
- What is that to us? (Matthew 27:4)

While the questions aren't strictly rhetorical, the motive behind each is clear: "Hey, that's not my job." Avoiding personal responsibility—for finding a missing brother, helping a crime victim, or setting right a cruel injustice—is the goal.

It's easy to look at the people who asked those particular questions and "just know" we would never do the same thing if we were in their shoes. Yet we are in *our* own shoes and right there, a spiritually pressing question lays constantly at our feet: *Will we help those suffering people it is within our power to help?*

The day in 2008 I asked that question of myself and the people at North Point Church, it began turning our church's world upside down—for the better. I asked it only after I was convinced in my own heart and soul that I would face the answer without any defensive questions of my own. The answer I got made me realize our church was headed straight into the Bermuda Triangle when it came to our missions and outreach efforts.

I realized we were in trouble and began to pray about our church's need in this area. I say "our church's need" because serving the poor and suffering isn't just about meeting their needs, it's about meeting our own needs to be obedient to Christ and fulfilled in our Christian living.

I combed through the Bible in search of guidance, and after a few days, I knew exactly what was wrong with our mission and outreach efforts: We were not being *strategic* with our finances, time, and energy when it came to reaching out. Sure, we were giving here and there, and some in our church helped around the community and on short term mission projects. But rather than focus on priorities to which we felt God calling our people, the work amounted to just a little bit of this and a little bit of that. We followed our whims instead of a winning strategy.

As I pondered this reality and prayed for direction, I felt that God showed me four global giants He wanted us to do battle with:

- DISEASE
- POVERTY
- ILLITERACY
- SPIRITUAL EMPTINESS

These Goliaths needed to be confronted, and God was asking North Point Church to take them on. I realized, though, that if we did, we would no longer be able to abide by old-school church outreach practices. Too often, "standard procedure" had left us wondering where our financial contributions were being sent and how they were being used. No, if we were to be strategic in fighting these four enemies, we could no longer sit by hoping someone else would use our resources well while our community went to pot.

We would use our money strategically. The battle would require focused effort and maximum efficiency, so instead of replicating the programs of others on our side in the fight, we determined to invest in and align ourselves with local and international organizations already confronting the same global giants God had called us to fight.

We committed to a journey that would yank us out of our comfort zone and see us join the fray. The battles would require us to put our finances, influence, gifts, energy, and talents on the line for one simple reason—because doing that is what Jesus would do:

> Speak up for those who cannot speak for themselves, for the rights of all who are destitute. Speak up and judge fairly; defend the rights of the poor and needy. (Proverbs 31:8-9)

A Bad Time for Good Works

Just as I began to face *the* question—in September 2008—the economy had tanked, unemployment was skyrocketing, and the housing market collapsing. The last thing any reasonable church leader would ask his or her members would be to give beyond their tithe for anything. But encouraging my people to give to help the hurting and impoverished, I believed, was absolutely the right thing to do at exactly the right time in the life of our church. It may not have fit with the world economic scene, but it was precisely God's will for us. Generous giving would be the opening salvo in our war with the four global giants.

Since I intended that our new strategic outreaches would have an *impact* on those we touch, I dubbed our initiative ImpACT (how clever of me!). But the importance of the concept lay in its two-pronged approach—its implications for the church and for the individuals in the church. The church together would:

- Influence for those who have no influence
- Mitigate spiritual emptiness
- Partner with social justice organizations
- Assist the poor
- Care for the sick and diseased
- Teach literacy

The individuals in our congregation would have the chance to "do something" about the four big problems, to respond to God's call to each of them to help. Each participant would be able to say "I ACT" to do my part. To make clear what we were asking of everyone involved, we provided a 3-step pledge card outlining their commitment (see Appendix 3). This sort of tool will increase the traction you get with those who want to help.

As I went public and rolled out ImpACT, I saw that I was onto something. For three weeks in a row, I preached the case for fighting the global giants. I told the church we had to throw everything we had at the beasts if we wanted to defeat them. And guess what? They got it!

People didn't seem to care that there were costs associated with our new outreach or that they were actually going to have to get their hands dirty to make it work. I saw ordinary people become convinced that together they could do extraordinary things to transform our community and world.

I do admit that, before starting my ImpACT series, I was apprehensive about talking as much about money as I knew I would have to. I had always hesitated to bring up the subject of giving because of the potential "turn off" it could be to unchurched visitors that might be in the congregation on any given Sunday. The last thing any seeker wants to hear their first time in church is a pastor asking for money! But when it came time to ask for the ImpACT pledge, I overcame my apprehension and did it boldly.

"The Church has dragged its feet getting on board with the issues that are robbing people of their lives, dignity, and quality of life—especially when it comes to AIDS," I told the congregation. "We need to fight these things!"

I scanned my listeners. Everyone nodded in agreement—even the unchurched visitors! They recognized I was asking for money to help the hurting people in our community, not to build an empire for our congregation. That's when I realized I was onto something bigger than just me or our local church.

But I didn't leave it at just giving money. I dared to ask of my church an even more precious commodity—time! On the last week of my ImpACT series, I challenged everyone to take part in our monthly outreach events that I decided to call Second Saturdays (more cleverness!— guess when these events take place). I told the congregation the events would find us teaming up with social justice organizations such as Convoy of Hope (www.convoyofhope.org),

Boys & Girls Town (bgtm.org), and the AIDS Project of the Ozarks (aidsprojectoftheozarks. org), among others (see Appendix 2 for more about these organizations). We would finance Second Saturday with pledges from the congregation, and we would deploy *hundreds* of volunteers to a selected organization each month to do a four-hour project. The resulting energy and productive output would look like *Extreme Makeover: Home Edition*. Month by month, Saturday by Saturday, we would makeover the world around us.

In the days after I launched ImpACT, I realized that our congregation of 4,000-plus had embraced everything about it. People gave money. Hundreds signed up for our initial Second Saturday event, and a buzz began throughout the congregation and community that North Point Church was genuinely bent on making a difference in the world.

We had our answer to the question about responsibility for the poor and suffering.

The Life of Jesus—Among Us

To be sure, Jesus came to earth to lead eternal souls into heaven. But along the way, He did a lot of focusing on earthly needs. The Good News He preached was *holistic*. Along with meeting people's spiritual needs, He met their physical needs. He healed leprous skin, fed hungry stomachs, restored blind eyes, fixed paralyzed legs, and gave thirsty mouths something to drink.

Social justice? I think so. Ushering in the Kingdom of God? Absolutely. God's kingdom is not just in heaven, it's on earth, too, when followers of Christ make a difference and lives are transformed for eternity. The fight against earthly tragedies is part of moving forward the Kingdom of Heaven. Jesus did it. He wants us to live and act like He did:

> Defend the cause of the weak and fatherless; maintain the rights of the poor and oppressed. Rescue the weak and needy; deliver them from the hand of the wicked. (Psalm 82:3-4)

Love Your Neighbors—Even the Ones Outside Your Neighborhood

Jesus equated loving our neighbors with loving God. If we love God, we will express it by loving other people. Love of God and love of fellow human beings are intertwined. It may be relatively easy to love the neighbor who welcomes you to his lakefront cabin on weekends or brings you tomatoes from her garden. But your neighbor is also the poor family whose kids you don't want your kids to play with.

Helping those who are poor and suffering is not always easy. Sometimes in desperation for food and medical attention or in the excitement of seeing her child get a toy or a bike, she can get pushy and downright mean. Or overwhelmed by the generosity (perhaps even embarrassed), he may not thank you as profusely as you think you deserve. But at times like those, you have to train your eyes to see what Jesus sees. How is God working in their lives? How is He working in *you*?

As I said, this doesn't always fit with old-school church thinking, but then neither did Jesus. After having a meal with sinners and tax collectors, local Pharisees railed against Jesus for spending time with such losers. But Jesus doesn't let them get away with their self-satisfaction: "'It is not the healthy who need a doctor, but the sick,' He says. 'For I have not come to call the righteous, but sinners'" (Matthew 9:12-13).

In the confrontation, Jesus is not just telling the people who follow Him how to do ministry, He is *showing* them how to do it. Working outside the walls of the church of His day, He befriends sinners and hangs out with social rejects. He displays the power of God in the community so everyone can see the Kingdom of God at work. His example is just as crucial today. At North Point Church, we constantly remind people that helping those who are struggling with disease, poverty, illiteracy, and spiritual emptiness is loving our neighbors, is ushering in the Kingdom of God, is living like Jesus.

Marketing the ImpACT

In the weeks leading up to my announcement that the church would implement ImpACT, we aggressively marketed the initiative before the people even learned exactly what it was.

In advertising lingo, we launched a "teaser" campaign. We saturated our target market (the church) with promotional flyers, posters, and postcards (see Appendix 3). I stumped for ImpACT from the pulpit and hinted at it during sermons and in online postings.

On the first Sunday of my ImpACT series, we gave everyone who entered the Auditorium a flyer (see Appendix 3) outlining the major themes and points of ImpACT and how each person could play a part in fighting the four global giants. I explained the ImpACT concept and told about Second Saturdays. We also let the congregation know up front we were going to ask for a pledge on the last weekend of the series (see Appendix 3 Pledge Cards).

In the second and third weeks, we presented the needs that exist in our community. The problems aren't just "out there." In our own backyard, we face immense needs. The high school drop-out rate in Missouri is 31 percent, contributing significantly to the illiteracy epidemic.[2] And this coincides with poverty statistics. In the Ozarks, 150,000 people live on incomes below the poverty line.[3] Making the case close to home helped me convince everyone to detest the four global giants as much as I do, and throughout the church, we built a case for why everyone should get involved.

On the last week of the series, I presented the specific case for ImpACT once again. "The statistics are staggering, the needs are huge, and if everyone participates," I said, "the costs will be minimal." To underscore the gravity of the situation, I shared information like the notes below for each of the global giants.

DISEASE

- Approximately 50 percent of the world's population (3.3 billion) is at risk of malaria.[4]

2. "Missouri Dropout Prevention Summit Fact Sheet," Missouri Department of Elementary and Secondary Education, April 13, 2009, accessed September 6, 2010, http://dese.mo.gov/dropoutprevention/documents/dop_summit_fact_sheet.pdf.
3. "Ozarks Food Harvest Faces of Hunger," Ozarks Food Harvest, accessed September 25, 2010, http://www.ozarksfoodharvest.org/hunger.html.
4. "CDC –Malaria–Malaria Worldwide," Centers for Disease Control and Prevention, Global Health–Division of Parasitic Diseases, February 8, 2010, accessed September 17, 2010, http://www.cdc.gov/malaria/malaria_worldwide/index.html.

- Malaria kills nearly 1 million people each year—85 percent are children under 5-years old, for whom malaria is a leading cause of death. This accounts for roughly one in five deaths in sub-Saharan Africa.[5]
- More than 2,000 children die from malaria every day.[6]
- Over 2 million people die from AIDS each year.[7]
- Over 280,000 children die from AIDS every year.[8]

POVERTY

- According to World Bank Development estimates for 2008, 2.6 billion people worldwide live on less than $2/day.
- UNICEF reports that 22,000 children die every day due to poverty.
- Even intermittent hunger can lead to growth retardation, weakened immune system, obesity, limited cognitive development, and emotional problems.

ILLITERACY[9]

- 44 million American adults are unable to read a simple story to their children.
- 21 million Americans can't read at all, 45 million are marginally illiterate, and 50 million read so poorly that they are unable to perform simple tasks such as balancing a checkbook and reading prescription drug labels.
- 20 percent of American high school seniors can be classified as functionally illiterate at the time they graduate, meaning they are unable to read their own diplomas.
- 70 percent of prisoners in state and federal systems can be classified as illiterate.

5. "Malaria." Worl Vision. Web. 10 Feb. 2010. <http://www.worldvision.org/resources nsf/main/press-image/$file/malaria-campaign.pdf>.

6. Ibid.

7. "Anova Health at the ISFIT Student Festival – News – Anova Health Institute." Anova Health Institute. Anova Health Institute, 22 Feb. 2011. Web. 18 May 2011. <http://www.anovahealth.co.za/news/entry/anova_health_at_the_isfit_student_festival/>.

8. Ibid.

9. "2003 National Assessment of Adult Literacy," US Department of Education, Institute of Education Sciences, National Center for Education Statistics.

- To determine how many prison beds will be needed in future years, at least one state (Arizona) bases projections in part on how well current elementary students perform on reading tests.
- Illiteracy and low literacy cost American businesses and taxpayers $20,000,000,000 a year.

SPIRITUAL EMPTINESS

- 14.7% of the world's population is either atheist or non-religious.[10] An additional 52.3% claim some religion other than Christianity.[11]
- Among American adults who have been married, one-third have experienced at least one divorce.
- Every year, nearly one million people die from suicide—a global mortality rate of 16 per 100,000, or one suicide death every 40 seconds.[12]
- In the last 45 years, suicide rates have increased by 60 percent worldwide.[13] It is among the three leading causes of death for those aged 15-44 years in some countries and the second leading cause of death in the 10-24 years age group. These figures do not include suicide attempts which are up to 20 times more frequent than completed suicide.

I reviewed the four global giants and explained how we would enter into strategic partnerships with social justice organizations both at home and abroad through our Second Saturday outreaches:

> Every month we will resource efforts to fight disease, illiteracy, poverty, and spiritual emptiness. We need 100 percent involvement in your giving and volunteerism. Give joyfully and sacrificially. Expect the unexpected from God, and know that your ImpACT pledge is over and above your regular tithe.

---

10. "Statistics on Religion in America Report –Pew Forum on Religion & Public Life," Religion in American Culture–Pew Forum on Religion & Public Life, Pew Forum on Religion & Public Life, August 30, 2011, http://religions.pewforum.org/affiliations.
11. "Top Ten Organized Religions of the World," Infoplease: Encyclopedia, Almanac, Atlas, Biographies, Dictionary, Thesaurus, accessed September 17, 2010, http://www.infoplease.com/ipa/A0904108.html.
12. "CDC–Home Page - Suicide–Violence Prevention– Injury," Centers for Disease Control and Prevention, accessed September 17, 2010, http://www.cdc.gov/ViolencePrevention/suicide/index.html.
13. Ibid.

I then asked everyone to prayerfully consider what part each should play in attacking the giants. "Plan to give as much as you can, as quickly as you can," I said. "Together we can change our community and the world!"

I was stunned by the results.

CHAPTER 2
THE IMPORTANCE FOR YOUR CHURCH

In the Introduction, I pointed out that the real "pursuit of happiness" is not based on how much self-fulfillment you achieve by doing anything and everything you can think of to do for yourself. Rather, it comes from contributing to the happiness of others. The effect of focusing outward instead of inward can be amazing.

North Point took the point in fighting the giants of oppression. And the energy released both inside and outside the church was remarkable. I thought I had already caught the vision, but when I saw the people in my congregation respond as they did, my own vision soared. Talk about a reason to get out of bed in the morning!

You may be looking for a way to revitalize your church. Perhaps ministry has gotten stale and needs a fresh start. Or maybe the growth you once experienced has simply stagnated. No matter what it is, reaching beyond the walls of your church and into the lives of those who are impoverished and hurting will transform you and your church, much for the better.

The reaction of my church to ImpACT nearly overwhelmed me. For sure, I had hoped the response would be positive, but the level of pledges and volunteerism amazed and puzzled me. "What," I wondered, "had been so lacking in us before that this idea received such an electrifying embrace from my congregation?"

After talking it over with some of my people and thinking about how the idea affected me when God first brought it to mind, I realized the need it met was simple. Somewhere along the line, our church lives had become dull and complacent relative to what power and excitement we saw witnessed in Scripture, and we all wanted a fresh start. In ImpACT, we recognized the potential for tapping into the magnificent working of God in a renewed and revitalizing way.

Give Until It Feels Too Good to Stop

Have you ever met a person who always gives to others and is miserable?

Neither have I.

The same is true of churches: Generosity = Happy Church; Stinginess = Unhappy Church. If your church only takes and does not give, you will eventually have a very unhappy group of people on your hands, with as many levels of dysfunction as you'd find at an Adams Family reunion.

The good news is that it's never too late to start giving. But ImpACT is not a temporary fix for the troubles you and your church may be facing. It's not a trendy organizational management tool or church growth technique. It's a transformation in the lifestyle of a church out of obedience to Christ.

ImpACT lies at the core of everything you and your church do and should be done with pure motives. The only goal is to help those in need and give a voice to the voiceless. This call to serve the needy should become part of the DNA of your church so that almost everything you do revolves around meeting the needs of those who are impoverished and suffering. If you do, the promise of God is big:

> Blessed is he who has regard for the weak; the Lord delivers him in times of trouble. The Lord will protect him and preserve his life; he will bless him in the land and not surrender him to the desire of his foes. The Lord will sustain him on his sickbed and restore him from his bed of illness. (Psalm 41:1-3)

Ever since ImpACT, North Point folks have given sacrificially of their time, energy, and finances to care for "the least of these" throughout our community. Because of it, lives have been transformed in our community and in our church. The way we do church has also changed.

We've reprioritized our goals and have spent time and money drilling down to the root problems affecting our community. As a result, people have been given help and hope, and children as well as adults see that a church in their community can be a safe, trustworthy place to explore spirituality and the claims of Christ. But I think we've been changed and refreshed more than anyone we've reached out to touch. We longed for a fresh start without even knowing it, and once it came our way, none of us would want to go back to how we were before.

Getting on Board with Hope

One of my favorite organizations is Convoy of Hope, which is a faith-based relief organization located in Springfield, Missouri, specializing in feeding the poor and suffering. Since Convoy of Hope started in 1994, it has served more than 35 million people in the United States and around the world through its feeding-the-children initiatives, community outreaches, disaster response, and partner resourcing.

During my tour of Haiti a few weeks after the 2010 earthquake with the organization's president and founder, we visited Port-au-Prince and saw many of the 25,000 school children Convoy of Hope feeds each day. In the days after the earthquake, Convoy distributed more than 9 *million* meals and thousands of water purification units and hygiene kits to people in need.

One of the things I love about Convoy of Hope is that they provide food, water and supplies to those in need without expecting anything in return. So far, they have distributed more than $200 million worth of food and supplies.

Check out www.convoyofhope.org for more information.

Time for Your Fresh Start?

Every church, regardless of its size or number of challenges it's facing, can be a church that makes an ImpACT! The question isn't "*can* your church do it?" The question is "*will* you do it?"

God yearns for His followers to be always faithful not only in our relation with Him, but in the vision He gives us for others. For every person who claims to be a Christ follower, sharing his or her faith is a part of that vision. There is no better way to share Christ's love with others than to serve them when they are in need:

> Therefore go and make disciples of all nations, baptizing them in the name of the Father and of the Son and of the Holy Spirit, and teaching them to obey everything I have commanded you. (Matthew 28:19-20)

ImpACT gives us the outlet to do just that.

Whatever your budget, staff resources, number of people in your congregation, or population of your community may be, your church can be actively involved in remedying some of your community's most pressing problems. By joining with local organizations bent on fighting the scourges that rob your neighbors of the peace and happiness Christ has for them, you will make an ImpACT. It will transform both the community and your church if you pursue *their* happiness.

CHAPTER 3
IMPRESS YOUR DETRACTORS

Did you know that if you make $25,000 per year, you are in an exclusive club of the top 11 percent of richest people in the world?[14] And if you make $40,000 a year, you're in the top 3 percent.

It's all relative, I know. If you're living on $25,000 a year in America you're squeaking by somewhere around or below the poverty line, subsisting on little more than the basics. But many of the basics we take for granted—clean water, shelter, and access to food—are luxuries only dreamt of by hundreds of millions of people around the world.

One of your biggest obstacles to helping these suffering masses will likely be the apathy that comes with the typical American middle-class comfort zone. It takes effort to see the need and even more effort to recognize that something can be done. But to be the loving extension of Christ that the Church is intended to be, we must help and care for those who are in need.

Be Boundless

In 2009, I was invited by the AIDS Project of the Ozarks to offer the invocation at a candlelight service in downtown Springfield in recognition of World AIDS Day. I was honored. One of the most powerful moments during the service came when those who were infected by AIDS came forward to share their stories. At one point, a gay man with tears in his eyes approached, hugged me, and thanked me for coming to pray. It was one of the most moving experiences I've ever had. Although some Christians might argue I shouldn't be encouraging people who have "brought such a curse upon themselves," I say: "Remember the Pharisees and Jesus' dinner with sinners."

---

14. Stearns, Richard, The Hole in Our Gospel (Nashville: Thomas Nelson, 2010), 215.

Too often, we draw boundaries between what we are and are not willing to do for those in need. Some seem to us to be worthy of help, others not so much so. But Jesus calls us to unbind our boundaries.

The same year I gave the invocation for the AIDS Day event, North Point Church gave the AIDS Project of the Ozarks its biggest donation from any organization for the year. That's the good news. The bad news is that we didn't give them all that much money. With what we gave, you might be able to purchase an average used car. Sad to think the organization thought we'd done so much!

I've found that once I embraced the principle of ImpACT, though, my awareness and understanding of others' needs has grown with each exposure to suffering. The candlelight service was no exception. As I stood among those gathered that night, I cried inside over all that needs to be done. Christ followers and the Church have immense opportunity to ameliorate the tragedy of AIDS, both locally and globally.

An estimated 40 million people are living with HIV/AIDS.[15] Sixteen million children have been orphaned by it, and in Africa alone, eight people are infected every minute with this unthinkable disease. Does Jesus care? Of course He does. So, should we? (This one *is* rhetorical.)

WWJD to fight AIDS/HIV? It's a question I've grappled with many times and one I've posed to everyone at North Point Church. Some respond that the fight against AIDS is not our fight. When I hear that, I think it sounds a lot like "who is my neighbor?" I can only shake my head because I know Jesus doesn't discriminate against sinners. He loves all of us and wants nothing more than for us to follow Him in helping anyone who needs the touch of His love.

Wave a White Flag

Surrender.

---

15.   "AIDS Project of the Ozarks Contents," AIDS Project of the Ozarks Home, AIDS Project of the Ozarks, accessed September 17, 2010, http://www.aidsprojectoftheozarks.org/contents/index/facts.

No one wants to give up. We'll do most anything to keep on having things our own way, but surrendering to the things of God has impressive results.

You become a Christ follower when you believe Jesus was the Son of God. But becoming a follower of Christ is a lifelong process of growing, learning, sacrificing, transforming, and change—all of which requires surrender. That's the crux of the problem for most us. Surrender is a battle for control. And giving up anything that we have control of is never easy, especially when it has to do with *our* relationships, *our* time, *our* finances, *our* habits, and *our* interests.

But surrender to God isn't like a bitter corporate takeover. While we do have to come to the point of wanting it His way, the best way to make that happen is to simply ask God to break our hearts with what breaks His heart—things like disease, poverty, illiteracy, and spiritual emptiness.

Recognize that Comfort Kills

> Fifteen thousand Africans are dying each day of preventable, treatable diseases—AIDS, malaria, TB—for lack of drugs that we take for granted.[16] This statistic alone makes a fool of the idea many of us hold on to very tightly: the idea of equality. What is happening to Africa mocks our pieties, doubts our concern and questions our commitment to the whole concept. Because if we are honest, there's no way we could conclude that such mass death day after day would ever be allowed to happen anywhere else. Certainly not North America or Europe, or Japan. An entire continent bursting into flames? Deep down, if we really accept that their lives—African lives—are equal to ours, we would all be doing more to put the fire out. It's an uncomfortable truth.[17]

Who said this? Not a church leader. Not a government official. Not even me. No, it was U2's front man and legendary rock star, Bono.

---

16. Stearns, The Hole in Our Gospel, 104.
17. Bono. (n.d.). BrainyQuote.com. Retrieved May 9, 2011, from BrainyQuote.com Web site: http://www.brainyquote.com/quotes/quotes/b/bono412285.html

Hands of Hope in Haiti, Young Strength at Home

The Convoy of Hope children's feeding initiative provides food for more than 11,000 children every day in Haiti alone. When I traveled there to see the work first hand, every Haitian I met had lost a family member or friend in the January 2010 earthquake. I also visited survivors' homes that were no bigger than the shed where I store my lawnmower and rakes.

We have it good in the United States. So good, that I was glad to have experienced Haiti because it shocked me and reminded me that other people's suffering should change us for the better. As the leader of your church, seeing for yourself how poverty, despair, hunger, and spiritual emptiness can negatively affect people is important when you're fostering vision in your people for those who are suffering.

Some of your church's most valuable assets are people in their twenties. The Church must embrace these young adults and find ways to accommodate their desire to worship in a setting they can relate to. Twenty-somethings will pump energy, ideas, creativity, and passion into your church. Are you doing everything to engage and utilize them? Give them an open door to connect spiritually and to exercise their social consciousness and they will buy into your church, its mission, and its heart for helping the people of your community.

So why aren't we doing more to put out the fire of poverty, disease and death that Bono speaks of in Africa? I believe it's because we're too comfortable! Think of all the stuff in your life meant for comfort: your job, house, cars, boats, clothes, big screen TV, investments, friends, hobbies, and money.

Most of these things bring us a certain level of security, entertainment, happiness, or contentedness. But the only thing that brings true happiness, security, peace, and comfort is giving everything to the Lord. That means living our lives for others, making a difference and realizing that the world's problems are our problems. Preoccupation with our own comfort leaves the world's chronically "uncomfortable" people alone to die.

In the book of Exodus, God reveals Himself to Moses in the form of a burning bush. He tells Israel's leader-to-be to go to Egypt and demand that Pharaoh let the Israelites go to the land God intends to give them.

Now if God were to come to you in that way, you'd think you would have the boldness to do whatever He directs—but not Moses. No, Moses has gotten settled quite nicely into a satisfying life with his wife, Zipporah, and the family flocks. Why shake things up by going back to the Egypt he was glad to have escaped? Why leave his comfort zone?

Despite the dramatic burning bush thing and what we might imagine to be our reaction, we're not so different from Moses. The problem he had was that he was afraid to surrender everything—to surrender even his comfort zone. So Moses argues with God (Exodus 4:10-13):

> I have never been eloquent, neither in the past nor since you have spoken to your servant. I am slow of speech and tongue.
>
> The LORD said to him, "Who gave man his mouth? Who makes him deaf or mute? Who gives him sight or makes him blind? Is it not I, the Lord? Now go; I will help you speak and will teach you what to say."

Besides assuring Moses he'll do fine in the speech-giving department, God even gives him the ability to work some miracles. Fun stuff like morphing a staff into a snake, transforming his own hand from normal to leprous to normal again, and turning water into blood. Finally, Moses is out of excuses and resorts simply to a whimpering request:

> But Moses said, "O Lord, please send someone else to do it."

God is undeterred. He knows surrender is the best thing for Moses. He also knows Moses doesn't have to be special—just surrendered. By enabling Moses to perform miraculous signs, God tells Moses, the Pharaoh, Israelites, and the world, that He can take the common and do the uncommon, the extraordinary, with it.

The same is true with each of us. When we surrender our relationships, time, material possessions, interests, habits, and things of value to Him to fight the four global giants, we put ourselves in a sweet spot where untold good things can result.

It's amazing how many people emulate Moses even when opportunities are leaping out at them from every angle. Common refrains you'll hear from people you try to enlist in ImpACT might be:

- "I don't have the right skills or abilities."
- "God can't use someone like me."
- "I'm not spiritual enough."
- "I don't have the right education."
- "I'm not smart enough."
- "I don't have enough money to be of any use to God."

When people indulge in such excuses, they miss the point of 2 Corinthians 12:9: "But he said to me, 'My grace is sufficient for you, for my power is made perfect in weakness.'" Same as the Moses message: It's up to God to provide the power, not you.

Despite this promise, many people implode because of insecurities and lack of confidence in the abilities and talents God has given them. Moses was just like us, but he eventually came around. When he did, God used him to part the Red Sea with his staff and bring down manna from heaven that sustained the Israelites for 40 years in the wilderness.

To do extraordinary things, all God needs is available and obedient people. God does not call the equipped; He equips the called.

How to Handle an I-can't-do-it Personality

Every church leader will have to deal with someone who seems to have more time to make up excuses than it would take to simply get out and serve. Here are some common excuses we've heard from people who say they can't help with Second Saturday events—along with some great suggestions on how to respond.

Excuse: I don't have transportation.
Response: No worries. Just get to the church, and we'll get you to the site.

Excuse: I can't make it because I have to watch the kids.
Response: No problem. They can come to the onsite events—there are at least a couple each year, so they can get involved too!

Excuse: I don't have time.
Response: Then you must think it takes longer than it really does. The time requirement is only four hours, once a month. Guaranteed!

Excuse: I might get bored.
Response: Ha! I doubt that. Everything's arranged so the events are loads of fun, and you get to meet great new people while you make an ImpACT!

Excuse: I can't stand for long or sit for long. And I'm claustrophobic, too. (Yes, we've really heard this one!)
Response: There's a way for everyone to work, no matter what your limitations might be. Each event involves different tasks, and we'll find something you can do—sitting, standing, indoors, outdoors. You'll be amazed at how productive you feel.

Help the Poor Always—and Then Some

When North Point was sizing up the global giants, we learned some startling facts such as:

- 3,611 people die of treatable childhood diseases each day[18]
- 85 percent of all juvenile offenders rate as functionally or marginally illiterate[19]
- 1 out of 10 households in the United States either experience hunger or are at risk of hunger[20]
- 30,000 people die *every day* from hunger-related problems.[21]

The problems may be staggering, but Jesus never backed away from troubles. He even admitted to the disciples "the poor you will always have with you" (Matthew 26:11). Yet despite the immensity of the problem, the mandate to help is equally clear from Scripture: "He who oppresses the poor shows contempt for their Maker, but whoever is kind to the needy honors God" (Proverbs 14:31).

By facing up to the issues, you'll grasp the gravity of the battle and find inspiration to provide solutions. Mother Teresa, one of the most famous poverty-fighters of all time, considered herself a small tool in God's hand: "I am a little pencil in the hand of a writing God who is sending a love letter to the world."[22] Yet she achieved world-changing results for the needy.

By fighting the ever-present giants, we keep poverty from getting worse wherever we serve, we save individual lives that might otherwise be lost, and we show the world that followers of Christ care and are resolved to live out their faith no matter what the odds. Jesus wants to help every person on this earth who is suffering, impoverished, thirsty, and hungry. He

---

18.   Stevens, Philip, "Diseases of Poverty," International Policy Network, 2004, accessed September 10, 2010, http://www.who.int/intellectualproperty/submissions/InternationalPolicyNetwork.pdf.
19.   "2003 National Assessment of Adult Literacy."
20.   Ozarks Food Harvest, accessed September 13, 2010, http://www.ozarksfoodharvest.org/index.html.
21.   "Facts on World Hunger and Poverty - a Problem That Could Readily Be Solved." Change.net - Home * Powered by Hearts & Minds - Information for Change * End Poverty Now. Hearts and Mind Network, July 2001. Web. 30 Aug. 2011. <http://heartsandminds.org/poverty/hungerfacts.htm>.
22.   Teresa Calcutta. (n.d.). Great-Quotes.com. Retrieved December 9, 2011, from Great-Quotes.com Web site: http://www.great-quotes.com/quote/6155

wants to be their Savior, and He wants to walk with them through their darkest days. And He can do that faster and on a wider scale if you get involved.

Admit that Some May Be Guilty

It's easy to condemn people the moment we set eyes on them. Many otherwise well-meaning people turn a blind eye to suffering people because they figure those folks brought it on themselves by their own bad behavior or poor decisions or lack of discipline or failure to take responsibility for themselves. I've looked many people in the eye who make these objections and offered two simple words in response: So what?

We're all human and have inherent flaws. Each of us would do well to remember the truth of "there but for the grace of God go I."

Jesus, who has every right to judge anything and anyone in the universe, never rushed to judge a hurting soul. Poor, suffering, illiterate, diseased sinners were recipients of His grace and love, not His condemnation. Rather, He used their need to demonstrate His power to change lives, minds, and hearts. We should do the same.

And believe me, I'm not saying this with the naiveté to suggest that everyone you serve is worthy or that no one will take advantage of your kindness. I've encountered both—more than once. Each year, a handful of unscrupulous people take advantage of our kindness by returning the toys, bikes, and school supplies we've given their children back to the stores where they came from. But even so, if a kid comes to our church, receives a bike, interacts with Christ followers, and gets a glimpse of a church filled with loving and caring people, that might be just the seed to someday draw him or her to Christ. And that's a win—even if their parents do swap the bike for cash at the local Walmart.

I can say equally emphatically, though, that many more people *won't* abuse your loving acts. A few bad apples shouldn't keep you from the rich harvest in your community.

Accept Doubt and Run with It

Have you ever heard a preacher say, "You've got to know that you know that you know"? This means that when in doubt, work yourself into an emotional frenzy that leads to some degree of certainty. Wow. When you first hear that, it really sounds great, a bedrock faith, right? How about: Wrong-O! I've concluded that the saying is a load of…well, manure.

There is no way to always, in every situation, every day, know that you know that you know. I wish there was, but that's just not how God—in His wisdom, I presume—has allowed it to be. Biblical scholar Frederick Dale Bruner says, "The Christian faith is bi-polar. Disciples live their life between worship and doubt, trusting and questioning, hoping and worrying."[23]

Doubt is not just a contemporary problem, either. In Matthew 28 there is a statement that absolutely blows me away: "Then the eleven disciples went to Galilee, to the mountain where Jesus had told them to go. When they saw him, they worshiped him; but some doubted."

Some doubted? What! How can that be! These guys had been with Jesus for three and a half years. They saw Him walk on water, raise dead people, and heal the blind. They saw Him get crucified and then come back to life, "*but some doubted*." Amazing! Beyond amazing, in fact.

Seeing that doubt can happen even to people with first-person experience of Jesus, my conclusion is this: Authentic faith does not mean you will be doubt-free; doubt is an inescapable part of the human condition. Like it or not (and I don't), doubt is a part of being human. If you wait until all doubt is removed before you commit to something, you will never get married, take a job, have a child, make a friend, follow God, or help those in need.

God is not intimidated by your honest questions. He does not call anyone to leave their intellect at the door, and Jesus never said, "Choose between me or the truth." He tells us to seek truth because it will set us free. An honest pursuit of truth will eventually lead to Him. Yes, the disciples doubted and wrestled with their faith even after they had spent time with

---

23.   In J. Ortberg. *Faith & Doubt*. Grand Rapids, MI: Zondervan, 2008, 176.

Jesus and had front row seats for His extraordinary life. But at the end of the day, their doubt led to a stronger faith that would eventually change the world.

The same is true for you. Doubt can lead to stronger faith. You may question whether embracing ImpACT will change your church and your community, but you'll never know until you try it. Yes, you will run into challenges, detractors, and setbacks that cause your faith to waiver. But if you stick with it, keep asking honest questions and looking for ways to figure things out, you, too, will eventually help change the world. Only seeing it in action can erase or minimize your doubt.

One particular doubt often creeps in with some churches. They're afraid they don't have the necessary resources—money, size of facility, number of people available. But guess what: North Point Church started small, and since we started ImpACT, our church has experienced severe growing pains (see Appendix 7 for direction on how the program can be modified depending on the size of your church).

Currently, we are blessed with nearly 5,000 people each weekend. *Outreach* magazine has called us one of the fastest growing churches in the United States, but we are a megachurch in need of more room. We're also a megachurch that knows its priorities. We'd rather help build God's kingdom by investing our finances, time, and energy into our community than into bigger and better facilities. As a result, on any weekend, you can choose from eight services on two different church campuses.

There are always alternatives to facilitate growth besides constructing bigger buildings. North Point is moving toward multi-site campuses and also utilizing television. One of our main lessons learned through our growth by ImpACT is that just because you grow, doesn't mean you need to go into a lot of debt to build. Remember, God is the source of our power, not our ability to cobble together resources, facilities, and people.

One Final Test

After all other arguments on behalf of the poor are laid out, one last test of what you should do sums up everything there is to be said: If you were suffering, how would you want to be treated? Your willingness to help the poor and needy may well be the greatest application ever of the Golden Rule.

CHAPTER 4

IMPLANT YOUR VISION

Warren Buffet, one of the most successful investors in the world, knows what it takes for a company to perform well. He believes corporate insiders need to have some "skin in the game."[24] What he means is that high-ranking company officials should have their own money invested in company stock. That way, if the company loses, they lose, and if the company wins, they win. It's the best motivation there is to assure commitment and effort.

Although I'm no Warren Buffet, I recognize the truth of what he's saying. As a result, I started wondering how much better a pastor might lead a church if he had something at stake, too. Since North Point Church was founded in September 2003, we have given out shoes, backpacks, and school supplies to kids. We've provided children with bikes and toys and their families with meals and a bevy of free health services. We also did public school makeovers in some of our community's poorest areas, and as our church started dipping its foot into the deep end of compassion work, I realized quickly that any church leader who is serious about helping the poor had to have some skin in the game.

Your skin in the game might mean finding the fortitude to buck tradition and be at odds with your board. Or it might mean that the first community outreach your church does is financed primarily by you. It might mean that people outside your church must become just as important to you as the people inside your church (talk about leaving your comfort zone!). Or it might mean you have to finally stand up to some ornery people in your church and tell them to get on board with the vision or move on to another congregation.

---

24.   Investopedia, dictionary, www.investopedia.com/terms/s/skininthegame.asp.

Easy Does(n't) It

You'll notice I haven't yet mentioned that embracing biblical social justice is an easy undertaking. There's a reason for that. Very few things about this are easy, but none of it is impossible. God has an inspired vision for those in your community who are mired in poverty and pain. If you've got the determination and fortitude to change your church and community by reaching out to the poor and suffering, He will also reveal His specific plans on how to meet needs in the neighborhoods that surround your church. Hopefully, He will use this book to help you discern those plans.

By making a bold move to give a voice to the voiceless and influence to those who lack it, you'll see God move in ways you've never thought possible. Don't be surprised if your church and finances grow. Don't be alarmed when people in your church step up and go all out to make a difference in your community.

As you meet needs, you'll see opportunities for you and your church to share Christ's message of love and hope with people you might not have ever had contact with. If you're up to the challenge and want nothing more than to take the gospel into your community by helping those in need, you'll be taking the first steps on a journey that will inspire your people, transform your church, and ImpACT your community.

Embrace Your Inner Rock Star

As I pointed out in Chapter 3, U2 front man Bono demonstrates a passion for helping the poor that Christ followers would do well to emulate. If it takes being a rock star to figure out how the Church should be giving a voice to the voiceless, we need to have more rock stars like Bono. He tells a revealing story of his own spiritual journey and how service to the poor got his attention:

> But then my cynicism got another helping hand. It was what Colin Powell, a five-star general, called the greatest W.M.D. of them all: a tiny little virus called AIDS. And the religious community, in large part, missed it. The ones that didn't miss it could only see it as divine retribution for bad behavior. Even on children...

even though the fastest growing group of HIV infections were married, faithful women.

Aha, there they go again! I thought to myself, judgmentalism is back! But in truth, I was wrong again. The Church was slow, but the Church got busy on this, the leprosy of our age. Love was on the move. Mercy was on the move. God was on the move.[25]

That wasn't the case several decades ago when AIDS first began plaguing the earth. People were scared. Scientists and doctors were baffled. The gay community was reeling. And the Church? It went on the defensive, pointing out the moral disgrace that seemed to be the cause. Like Bono said, the Church was slow to see AIDS/HIV as a golden opportunity to share the love of Christ. At the time, the Barna Research Group took notice of this disturbing trend and asked evangelical Christians whether they would be willing to donate money to help children orphaned by AIDS. Only three percent of those polled answered that they would definitely help. Fifty-two percent said they *probably* or *definitely would not help*. Every other group surveyed (i.e., non-Christians) were more willing to contribute.[26]

Like Bono noted at the National Prayer Breakfast, things have changed in the Church regarding its stance on social issues since the early 1980's. Church leaders like Rick Warren, Bill Hybels, and others have helped move the Church out of its walls and into the needy masses against the scourges of hunger, disease, and poverty. When it comes to AIDS—which some pastors publicly said was God's punishment on homosexuals—there are now many churches helping sufferers, conducting health education workshops, and undergirding ministries that care and treat those infected by the disease.

But there is still much work to be done. The statistics remain grim: Every 12 seconds, someone dies because of AIDS/HIV.[27] By finally taking the initiative to help fight the AIDS pandemic, though, the Church has not only done the right thing, it has gained the respect

---

25. Bono, speech at National Prayer Breakfast, 2006.
26. In Richard Stearns. *The Hole in Our Gospel,* World Vision 2009.
27. "Global Crisis | Global Solution | Global Leader," © 2011 International AIDS Vaccine Initiative, accessed January 2011, http://www.iavi.org/Lists/IAVIPublications/attachments/5b6eea30-490d-4cce-889e-ed9012b44f55/IAVI_Global_Crisis_Global_Solution_Global_Leader_2011_ENG.

of countless people. A couple years ago, I heard Bono tell Bill Hybels at a leadership summit that Hybels and other Christians were messing Bono up because of the good work that was being done. He was being forced to change (for the better) his long-standing perceptions of the Church.

Fight the Good Fights

A lot of "causes" in the Christian community are nothing more than energy wasters, distractions from the central work churches should be about doing. Every Christmas, for instance, I hear well-intentioned people trying to bully retailers into having their employees use the greeting, "Merry Christmas" instead of "Happy Holidays." It may make us feel better to hear a more forthright acknowledgement of Christ's place in the season, but it really doesn't count for much in spreading the Kingdom of God.

Why do I say that? Because the secularization and commercialization of Christmas happened long ago. I believe it's pointless to waste time and influence on frivolous things like employee greetings at Best Buy and Walmart. The materialism will continue to motivate the stores and their customers, no matter what anyone says to you at the checkout counter. It's a ridiculous, energy-sapping fight that, in the grander scheme of things, doesn't accomplish anything that really matters.

If the Church is going to rise up and be vocal about what it is against, let's start with things like poverty, hunger, disease, spiritual emptiness, and illiteracy. It will give you results you can see, and you'll be thankful to God you were part of helping. North Point Church certainly has been.

The North Point ImpACT in 2009

During our first full year of doing ImpACT, we assisted several social justice organizations to help thousands of local residents crushed by poverty. A crucial part of communicating the vision for ImpACT is to celebrate the hard work, time, sacrifice, and finances our people have given. And one of the best ways to do that is to show your people exactly what they've accomplished. As an example, I've listed our tally below.

In late December 2009, we distributed a flyer (Appendix 3) to every person who came into our church to describe what we had accomplished during our first year of ImpACT, and this is what our people had to celebrate:

- Partnered with Rural Compassion, Ozarks Literacy Council, Victory Mission, AIDS Project of the Ozarks, Boys & Girls Town, Boys & Girls Club, Springfield Public Schools, OACAC, and Convoy of Hope;
- Gave out more than 600 pairs of shoes, socks, and underwear;
- Funded AIDS Project of the Ozarks to supplement their medical work;
- Served over 4,000 hot dogs, cookies, and chips meals to children and their families in need;
- Painted Victory Mission Trade School classrooms and dorm rooms;
- Gave out more than 1,000 bags of groceries;
- Provided books for 2 rural libraries;
- Put together 400 relief buckets for disasters;
- Provided a cleaning makeover for 71 bathrooms at The Missouri Hotel for indigent people (part of The Kitchen) and provided them with towels, wash rags, and toiletry items;
- Gave more than 7,000 books to children and their families;
- Supplied 100 new beds, bedding, and a bag of goodies and hygiene items for children at Boys & Girls Town;
- Handed out 195 swimsuits and beach towels for kids at Boys & Girls Club;
- Gave more than 150 haircuts and 50 medical exams;
- Funded The Kitchen to add on to its women's dorm;
- Supplied other organizations with clothing, food, and books;
- Provided a school makeover to a local school—painting classrooms, washing windows, trimming trees, painting playground equipment, and supplying mulch and new basketball backstops;
- Donated and sorted 8,000 pounds of clothing;
- Furnished 75 baby gates, 10 toddler cots, fifty 30-gallon totes and a commercial dryer to The Kitchen;

- Cleaned and painted Cook's Kettle Restaurant. Cook's Kettle is a Social service initiative operated by Victory Trade School, a 12-month program to prepare students for careers in the hospitality industry. (Cook's Kettle provides hands-on experience for trade school pupils and free meals for needy people in the community. VTS graduates receive a diploma from the National Restaurant Association Educational Foundation—see more at www.victorymission.com.)
- Contributed financially to other organizations at home and abroad.

Not bad for one year. Focus on the real priorities, and you can have a fulfilling list of your own.

CHAPTER 5

IMPROVE THE WAY YOUR CHURCH SERVES OTHERS

Our list of accomplishments hasn't always been especially "fulfilling." One Sunday early on, we passed out flyers asking for volunteers to help in our children's programs. We were looking for volunteers who would commit one hour every other week—just two hours a month. During each worship service, I held up the flyer and emphasized how important it is for people to take ownership of church ministries. I eloquently encouraged the vision for helping kids and just knew the congregation would be so inspired they could hardly keep their seats. It seemed to me a no-brainer that thousands of flyers supplemented with my ever-so-articulate encouragement would easily garner hundreds of volunteers.

There weren't even ten.

That day, I either flunked Congregational Communication 101 or our flyer read like Chinese. I didn't know which it was, but both had failed miserably. Nothing motivated the folks in our church.

Puzzling over the lack of enthusiasm for our kids' ministry, I began to suspect that we had become a church full of consumers who wanted to *be* served rather than to serve. The thought grated on me to no end because I had been teaching the merits of volunteerism ever since we had started the church. It should have been ingrained in the DNA of our church by now.

A Warning from the Past

Scripture shows that God's people through the ages have had a chronic problem of avoiding service that truly pleased the Lord. It's small comfort if you're trying to get a church off "go" but it's instructive to understand God's perspective on people who don't really serve those who need it most.

In Isaiah 58:1-5, we get a picture of God's people totally missing the point. They're diligent in prayers, fasting, and religious ceremony, but they're puzzled by God's reaction. He doesn't seem to notice or care about their activities.

> Shout it aloud, do not hold back. Raise your voice like a trumpet. Declare to my people their rebellion and to the house of Jacob their sins.
>
> For day after day they seek me out; they seem eager to know my ways, as if they were a nation that does what is right and has not forsaken the commands of its God. They ask me for just decisions and seem eager for God to come near them.
>
> "Why have we fasted," they say, "and you have not seen it? Why have we humbled ourselves, and you have not noticed?"
>
> Yet on the day of your fasting, you do as you please and exploit all your workers. Your fasting ends in quarreling and strife, and in striking each other with wicked fists. You cannot fast as you do today and expect your voice to be heard on high.
>
> Is this the kind of fast I have chosen, only a day for a man to humble himself? Is it only for bowing one's head like a reed and for lying on sackcloth and ashes? Is that what you call a fast, a day acceptable to the Lord?

What comes next is stunning. And if churches today took it to heart, this passage could re-shape Christianity. In Isaiah 58:6-7 we learn that God does not care so much about our fasts, traditions, facilities, Bible memorization, or even how long we've been Christ followers:

> Is not this the kind of fasting I have chosen: to loose the chains of injustice and untie the cords of the yoke, to set the oppressed free and break every yoke? Is it

not to share your food with the hungry and to provide the poor wanderer with shelter—when you see the naked, to clothe him, and not to turn away from your own flesh and blood?

These words describe a people who should be characterized by justice, fairness, and a concern for the poor. It's a holistic gospel, and if we get it right, God offers an amazing promise. In his book *The Hole in our Gospel*, Richard Stearns, president of World Vision, describes what will happen:

> When the hungry are fed, the poor are cared for, and justice is established, He will hear and answer His servants' prayers; He will guide them and protect them, and they will be a light to the world.[28]

This would make Christians irresistible.

Motivating the Motivations

So what could I do to get my church out from behind our own walls and into real service to God? I decided it was time for a very direct approach.

The week after I crashed and burned at raising children's program volunteers, I told our people that the health of our church isn't solely the responsibility of the pastoral staff.

"If you call NPC your home, it's on your shoulders," I challenged. "You're going to have to take ownership. If all you do is come to a service and leave, eventually this church is *done*."

I'm afraid it's just that cut and dried, and as a leader, it's your job to implore and empower your people to shoulder their rightful responsibility to grow and nurture the church.

"If you don't give, serve, and commit to this church, then who will?" I asked the people that day. "If you care about this church, then find a place to serve—today! The responsibility is yours."

---

28.   Richard Stearns. *The Hole in Our Gospel,* World Vision 2009, 57.

To be what God wants us to be requires each of us to get beyond self-centeredness and ask God what He expects of us.

The world is attracted to God's concern for the poor. And when the Church expresses this concern and does something to counter the suffering of the impoverished, people sit up and take notice and actually listen to what Christians are saying. Suddenly, the Church has an audience willing to listen to the best message ever shared, Christ's message of love and redemption.

To do this, we had to re-think some things at North Point and re-invent many of our attitudes, perspectives, and approaches to ministry. You'll probably have to do the same, so I'll spend the rest of this chapter talking about what some of those things may be.

Realize that Your Dreams Are Not Theirs

ImpACT is not about you, your church, your goals, or even the spiritual lives of the people in your church. Helping people and expecting nothing in return—giving God room to change people's lives—is *the* agenda. That will mean getting outside of yourself in many ways and recognizing that the people you serve likely have a very different vision of what matters than you do.

For the single mom trying to make ends meet, for instance, her dreams may not be yours. She's probably not thinking about where her children will go to college or whether the house she wants to buy someday will be in a good school district and convenient to a Super Walmart. Her biggest dream is probably nothing more than to have a bag of groceries for the hungry mouths she has to feed.

So how do you fulfill a dream like that?

During one of our first Second Saturday events (see Appendix 1, Glossary, about "Second Saturday"), we partnered with Convoy of Hope. For four hours on a Saturday morning, 450 volunteers from our church packed 8,000 bags of groceries, assembled 4,000 hygiene kits and 4,000 seed packet kits, and did grounds maintenance. Convoy of Hope distributed the items to thousands of needy people in the weeks after our Second Saturday. By helping Convoy of Hope, we reach the world. It's a great example of being efficient and strategic in meeting needs. There are organizations like Convoy of Hope whose work we can't replicate at the level they are doing it. But by coming alongside them, we accomplish our goal of reaching the world.

Helping social justice organizations can change the world—and along the way fulfill dreams like giving a single mom a bag of groceries, a toy, or a few school supplies. We give people a hand up to change their circumstances and rejuvenate their outlook on life.

Find Your Sweet Spot

Everyone can play a part in ImpACT. Someone on your staff or a volunteer might want nothing more than to set up and tear down the outreach event. Someone else might want nothing more than to plan the minutia of the outreach or market it in your community.

You might contribute best by casting vision for ImpACT and keeping it in front of your people by talking about it from the pulpit, Facebooking and Twittering it. Or you might be best suited to work alongside the volunteers in the trenches.

Facebook Updates and Tweets about ImpACT

Getting ready for 2nd Saturday in July! Don't forget to sign up.
www.northpointchurch.tv/impact

Making an ImpACT @ Boys & Girls Town in May. Sign up today!
www.northpointchurch.tv/impact

It's really up to you. But finding your sweet spot is crucial to the success of ImpACT. A great way to find it is to evaluate what you do every time you do it. That way, you discover what you do well naturally so as to hone your strengths. You also find out what doesn't come as naturally to you so you can shore up the weaknesses in your service.

After every Second Saturday outreach our team gets together and evaluates how we did and what we can do better next time to make our outreaches more efficient and effective. We ask honest questions, seek feedback from our guests, volunteers and the organizations we help, and look for ways to do everything better (see Appendix 4).

Seeking improvement every time out is crucial because ultimately we want to see lives changed for eternity. Knowing lives are on the line is reason enough to be at our best when we serve our community.

Evaluate and Recalculate

At the end of every Second Saturday, we ask our leaders several questions to gauge how the event went, what could be done better, where we had weaknesses, and what went right. Then we change what needs to be changed (see Appendix 4).

Knowing your downside is every bit as important as knowing what you do best. Taking an honest inventory of your church's weak points requires brutal honesty. You must look at everything you do with a critical eye. If something isn't working, get rid of it. If something kind of works, figure out how to make it better. If something works fine, determine how to replicate it in other areas of your church.

Discovering what your church is downright lousy at and fixing the problem is crucial to the success of ImpACT. At North Point Church, for example, we realized that our mid-week services produced "sideways energy" that didn't measure up to our standards of excellence. (Sideways energy means time-consuming but low-priority ministries.) For a while, we tinkered with them, trying to make them better, but eventually, we realized it wasn't working so…we got rid of them. No more mid-week services! Are you ready to be that radical if it means being more effective for God's kingdom? Get rid of sideways energy so your church can be focused.

Doing ImpACT takes lots of energy, finances, and focus. If something in your church is keeping you from doing ImpACT with excellence, evaluate it and fix it, or give it the ax.

Without a doubt, some things your church is currently doing will need to be reinvented, tweaked, upgraded, or dismissed. As a leader, your job requires the fortitude and bravery to make the necessary changes for the greater good of your church and community.

ImpACT is time consuming. You can't do everything as a church. Get rid of "sideways energy" so your church can be focused. You don't need things like that taking resources and people away from your commitment to ImpACT.

Create a Blended Family

Building a strong ImpACT-type outreach plan will work best if your church is home to individuals with a range of spiritual backgrounds. Too often churches are narrow in this regard, but every church should have a healthy ecosystem of mature believers, young believers, and non-believers. To keep that system in balance, your mature believers should regularly invite their unchurched friends to attend.

When a mature believer invests in a relationship and invites a friend to church (we call this "invest and invite"—more cleverness, right?), the church joins a unique partnership. The individual believer leverages his or her relationship with a non-believer to expose that person to the church experience. North Point, in turn, does everything in our power to provide an unforgettable experience once the unchurched person walks in the door. We want spiritual lights to turn on as we support the bridge-building between the mature believer and his or her friend.

The goal, of course, is not just to enroll another ImpACT worker but to set the stage for life change through Christ. When that happens, someone's eternity is resolved, and we usually get another person involved in ImpACT to boot—because that's often what most attracted the person to NPC.

A word of caution is in order about creating this sort of healthy mix of non-, new, and old believers. Sometimes "rookie" Christians need to be given some latitude that may stretch the veterans' tolerance a bit. Let me give you an example.

A friend of mine brought one of his unchurched buddies to North Point—a guy who was skeptical of church and ripe with negative preconceived ideas of what church would be like. But he was immediately impressed with how differently we did things. He exclaimed to my friend, "This is f---ing cool!"

Granted, his choice of words was out of place (even at our church), but it was music to my ears. His rich street language proved to me that we were doing things right. Our church impressed a guy who had never been in a church and had come ready to 'dis' anything he saw there.

When you embrace ImpACT, your church inherits a strand of DNA that transforms its culture. Suddenly, you're attractive to unchurched people who wouldn't give you the time of day otherwise. Rather than taking offense that someone dropped an f-bomb in your foyer, be prepared to rejoice that someone would give Jesus a couple of hours—perhaps for the first time—and would potentially take his first step on the path to heaven.

These are the kinds of people Jesus is looking for, and He wants you to do everything in your power to reach them. Keep that foremost in mind, and you won't have to be judgmental, push political views, or occupy a soapbox about all the things you're against. You can just love people the way Jesus did. Then step aside, and let the Holy Spirit do His work to bring God's family together in His way.

Throw Out the Old Rules

The rulebook for church that you grew up with or studied in Bible college has changed. Technology, the busyness of life, competing religions, and cultural distractions have put the squeeze on churches. But rather than getting into a funk and longing for the alleged glory days of old, ImpACT leaders embrace the new realities.

They utilize technology and innovations to tell an age-old story. Rather than waiting for people to come to their churches, they take their churches to the people. The message hasn't changed, but the methods have. ImpACT-style leaders welcome the new opportunities for reaching their communities for Christ and write their own rulebooks.

Are you clinging to tradition, comfort, a certain income level, or "the way things have always been done"? If so, the question you need to ask yourself is, "How long will this last?" I can tell you the answer: Not long. In a church where traditions and regulations trump authenticity and connectedness, bad things happen. Ultimately, the church dies.

When you embrace ImpACT, your church will take on a vibrancy and color that will draw people to it. You'll wake up each day, your mind whirring with possibilities and ideas that can potentially reach more people for Christ. God not only wants you fulfilling the Great Commission, He wants you excited, enriched, and yearning for more.

If that sounds good to you, then the best starting point is to throw your old rulebook out the window. Once you lose the old rules, of course, you're going to need to establish some new ways. Here are the top five I recommend:

> *(1) Associate, don't duplicate.* Since our community already had amazing social justice organizations fighting the global giants, we opted to support their work rather than compete with it by starting our own. The AIDS Project of the Ozarks was already set up to help people with AIDS, so by helping the AIDS Project, we fight AIDS in the most effective way we can. Our resources, experiences, and love support an already excellent work while we reach the community they serve with a lasting expression of Christ's love.

> *(2) Money can't buy you love, but sometimes it is enough to get the job done.* I know we're all used to challenging people to give more than just their money, but sometimes, money is exactly—and all—that is needed. At least three times a

year, we give funds to a local organization instead of our time simply because it's the best way to help. We see it as a great opportunity to benefit others through the financial resources God has given us. And besides, it also gives our staff and volunteers a much-deserved break. Don't ever apologize for raising resources. It takes money to help the poor!

(3) Even a little can be a lot. Eighteenth century statesman, author, and conservative political philosopher Edmund Burke claimed that "nobody made a greater mistake than he who did nothing because he could do only a little."[29] Americans need to take that message to heart because we tend to be extremists. People aren't satisfied with doing something everyone else can do, like running a measly 5k race. They want to do things that set them apart from the pack, like running a marathon through a desert in bare feet. While there is nothing wrong with setting a high bar, don't let great expectations keep you from helping the poor and suffering. If your church can do only a small outreach or write a small check to a local organization, do it! Just because you may not be able to do a massive ImpACT outreach that feeds thousands of needy people at your first event, that doesn't mean you should skip ImpACT. Do what you can, strive for excellence, and use the momentum you gain to do the next one even better.

(4) 30 or 300 ordinary people can do more than a few extraordinary people. You, your staff, and a handful of core church members might be extremely gifted, talented, and intelligent. But no matter how rare and extraordinary you are, you cannot do a good job on ImpACT alone. The first "law of ImpACT" is that 30—or 300—"regular people" who are passionate about helping the hurting will be way more productive and powerful than a handful of super-talented people. Plus, everyone gets their hands dirty, builds relationships, participates in something meaningful, and experiences firsthand the satisfaction of helping others. When you have 300 volunteers willing to give four hours (1200 person-hours!), you have an army of compassion that can change the world. If your church is smaller, you can partner with other churches or organizations to reach critical mass.

---

29.   Burke, Edmund. http://www.memorable-quotes.com/edmund+burke,a1064.html

(5) Give, live, and thrive. A.W. Tozer knew a church is more than just a collection of people under one roof: "One hundred religious persons knit into a unity by careful organizations do not constitute a church any more than eleven dead men make a football team. The first requisite is life, always."[30] If your church isn't a life-giving organization, it's as good as dead. Make sure you're doing everything in your power to keep your church out of the morgue. Stay Bible-based, keep Christ at the center of everything you do, value your staff and people, conduct Second Saturday outreach events, and do it all with Kingdom-of-God objectives in mind. Foster life so you can give life.

Tap the Power of Disillusionment

At the first church I served, the pastor and I were once called to an "emergency" board meeting. Church leaders were concerned about a horrendous change we had initiated. We discovered that our offense was that we had moved the pulpit from its original place in the sanctuary to a side room so we could make room for a more functional podium. By the time the board meeting ended, the pulpit had been returned to its "rightful" place, but rumors erupted about the new music volunteer being immoral, and seeds were sown in me that eventually led to my resignation.

I was disillusioned, but I quickly determined that, wherever I find myself, I will peel away any dysfunctional traditions that keep me or others from following Jesus. Far from undermining my faith and sense of mission, disillusionment fueled a passion to improve my service to the Lord. I stayed in ministry and began a search for ways to make church authentic, honest, and real. ImpACT is one of the results of that search. Disillusionment with people, projects, events, plans—even God—can lead to deeper and more significant transformations in your spiritual journey and service.

---

30. Tozer, A.W. http://www.goodreads.com/quotes/show/104214

Partners Worth Partnering With

Sometimes finding the right social justice organizations to partner with is like digging through a toolbox to find the right tool. To make the search easier, confine your thinking about potential partners to organizations who are already fighting the global giants.

Here are just a few organizations we have partnered with in the past couple of years (for more information on each, see Appendix 2):

- *Down Syndrome Group of the Ozarks* serves those with Down syndrome to provide support, education and more.
- *Convoy of Hope* works locally and globally to provide for those in need;
- *AIDS Project of the Ozarks* reaches out to people dealing with AIDS/HIV;
- *Chi Alpha* is an outreach to college students throughout the nation;
- *Boys & Girls Club* works with disadvantaged children to help them realize their potential for growth and development.

The bottom line for our partnerships is that we work with organizations that are making a difference and doing so effectively and efficiently.

Channeled in a healthy direction, disillusionment generates power to go against the grain of old ways of thinking and acting. For reasons I have never fully understood, many churches are enslaved to traditions, to mean people, modern-day Pharisees, and legalism. But Jesus never intended our churches to be dominated by such negative forces.

Two thousand years ago in Capernaum, Jesus crowded into a claustrophobic room with a mass of folks which ranged from those who believed His words were life to those who would just as soon kill Him. Some industrious men on the roof, determined to have Jesus help their friend, ripped open the structure and lowered their paralyzed comrade on a bed to Jesus.

As startling as their act must have been, Jesus wasn't fazed. He simply looked at the stricken man and said, "Son, you're sins are forgiven." With those words, Jesus declared Himself to be God, a radically against-the-grain position.

While you may not be healing paralytics, your work in ImpACT will likely go against the grain of what many people are used to. But your acts on behalf of the needy tell your community, "We are doing all we can to live like Jesus. That's why we put our time and money toward things churches don't normally do."

Take a Stand Against MDPs

Today:

- One billion people in the world do not have access to clean drinking water;[31]
- More than 25,000 children will die because of hunger or hunger-related causes;[32]
- 25 percent of the world's population earns $1 or less per day.[33]

Did I mention that the stakes are high?

Modern-day Pharisees (MDPs) can destroy your plans to help your community faster than a nuclear bomb. But you can't permit anyone to come between you and God's best for people in need. Identify your problem people and let them know as you begin ImpACT that their negativity and disunity are not welcome in your church. If they change, they can stay. If they don't, show them the door.

I offer the following intelligence to help you identify the MDPs among you:

- Fort builders who are good at building places where they and others like them are well received and included, but outsiders are rejected;

---

31. "Water Facts," Water.org, accessed September 17, 2010, http://water.org/learn-about-the-water-crisis/facts/.
32. Poverty.com–Hunger and World Poverty, accessed September 17, 2010, http://www.poverty.com.
33. "List of Countries by Percentage of Population Living in Poverty," Wikipedia, the Free Encyclopedia, accessed February 17, 2011. http://en.wikipedia.org/wiki/List_of_countries_by_percentage_of_population_living_in_poverty. [January 29, 2011.

- Big talkers who prattle about sharing their faith but show no real motivation to do it;
- Hypocrites who look down on those who don't know Jesus as their Savior;
- Cry babies who get agitated when other followers of Christ strive to reach out to the community;
- Traditionalists who cannot stand veering from the old ways, even if doing so means people will come to Jesus;
- Spiritual stiffs who detest extending grace and forgiveness because for some sick reason they don't believe anyone really deserves it—except for them;
- Micromanagers who believe their spirituality is based on works and deeds;
- Smooth talkers who say all the right things because they understand church doctrine, but they rarely do the right thing unless it is of some benefit to themselves;
- Know-it-alls who readily agree that only Jesus can save you from your sins but who insist they have all the rules everyone must follow to maintain that faith;
- Gossipers who take prayer requests and share the gory details with others under the guise of getting you the prayer you need;
- Wanna-be leaders who will tear a church apart if the pastor doesn't do it their way;
- People with blinders who believe and only embrace the parts of the Bible convenient to their worldview;
- Homophobes;
- Those dismissive of anyone who smokes, curses, watches R-rated movies, is divorced, or is pregnant out of wedlock;
- Folks living in denial of what they are (there's not a Pharisee alive that would admit to being a Pharisee);
- Delusional people, believing they are well balanced and liked;
- Judgmental people who embrace a standard of their own righteousness so as to use it as a way to judge others.

Anyone can change, of course, and you want to welcome any newness of heart, no matter what the initial disposition of the person. But the point is, you'll need to help the MDP's in your midst catch the vision for outreach in order to move ahead effectively.

CHAPTER 6

IMPROVISE FOR CHANGE

The movie *Braveheart* delivers a momentous truth when William Wallace (Mel Gibson) rallies his fellow Scotsmen to fight the English. Gathered at the edge of a battlefield, Wallace and his men are desperately outmatched by the gargantuan British army. They lack the military training and weapons for a proper battle, but Wallace is unfazed. He implores the men to fight alongside him. Finally, one soldier voices the fear in the minds of every man listening to Wallace's impassioned words.

Waving toward the British troops, the terrified man exclaims, "Against that? No, we will run, and we live."

Wallace pauses, nodding his head in apparent agreement. "Aye, fight and you may die," he responds. "Run and you will live—at least a while. And dying in your beds, many years from now, would you be willin' to trade *all* the days, from this day to that, for one chance, just one chance?"

The same is true in churches. If we run from those who are unchurched, we'll live for a while, but we'll eventually die. On the other hand, today—and the people in front of you right now—may be *your* chance to make a difference.

Look around. Some churches are on death's door. Statistics tell us that only 17 percent of Americans attend church, and each year, some 4,000 churches are shuttered.[34] This has to change. We need a revolution.

---

34. "How Many North Americans Go Regularly to Church?", Religious Tolerance, Ontario Consultants on Religious Tolerance, 2007, accessed September 27, 2010, http://www.religioustolerance.org/rel_rate.htm.

We must fight to become relevant to a culture that is abandoning us and use every means possible to reach unchurched people. If we do, we'll not only be helping change people's eternal destinations, we'll be doing exactly what Christ told us to do here on earth.

Before Jesus left this planet, he gave a Braveheart-esque speech. He said, "Go ImpACT your culture and make disciples" (my version of Matthew 28:19, by the way).

He didn't say, "Shutter the doors and windows on your church and keep outsiders away." He called His followers to make a difference, to be unselfish, to be accepting, and to do whatever it takes to reach unchurched people for Him. Sometimes things must collide for that to happen.

Be as Different as You Are One

If churches were party snacks, many of them would look like a can of Pringles®—every chip exactly the same color and size. The great thing about them is that they fit neatly in the container. But the church is not meant to be a closed container with all its people stuffed neatly inside. We're meant to be out in the culture making a difference for Christ. What churches should aspire to be is a bowl of Chex Mix®—all different shapes, flavors, and textures spread around in one delicious snack.

The Church is not supposed to be a place of blind conformity. God has provided, in the creative mix of people, an imaginative blend of skills, perspectives, and approaches to life. He's also given us the way—through unity in His Son—to be of one mind and heart in all we do. It's that beautifully diverse expression of Christ that can make the greatest impact in your community, but you need to nurture it to allow it to happen.

If some people assert that your church is a rightwing, fundamentalist, rule-following, clone machine, you might want to take a second look to see how Pringle-ish you are. Prepare yourself and your people to change. Once ImpACT starts its work in you, you'll grow into the Mix you're intended to be, and that will grow you into a more and more effective tool in God's hands. Then you'll see your church becoming what Paul talks about in 1 Corinthians

12:12: "The body is a unit, though it is made up of many parts; and though all its parts are many, they form one body. So it is with Christ."

Tip Some Cattle

Sacred cows are those processes, attitudes, or ways of doing things that an organization considers "untouchable." Most organizations have them, but they're rarely a healthy part of its make-up. In a church, those sacred cows range from rigid traditions to the encouraging of modern-day Pharisees to accommodation of mean-spirited people.

One problem with sacred cows is that they are dream killers. They suck the life out of leaders and their people. Yet too many people are unwilling to let go of the cows. To help them release their grasp, I often ask leaders this question: "What have your sacred cows done for you lately?"

I usually get a blank stare or a shrug of the shoulders in reply. They either don't want to let go or are afraid of the resistance they'll face if they try to clean out the barn.

Usually, sacred cows—like "the way we've always done it"—will undermine your attempt at ImpACT, so you're going to have to tip them out. If they aren't paying you or your church any dividends, they need to go. They're like having a 10-foot basketball hoop on an elementary school playground—they don't make sense and aren't very useful. They'll stifle the best of intentions and destroy your utmost efforts to do good in your community.

So tip a cow, save a dream…and maybe even some eternal lives.

Excellent Is as Excellent Does

At North Point Church, striving for excellence is a part of our DNA. The reason? People are attracted to excellence, and excellence is a reflection of Jesus Christ.

In *The Little Big Things: 163 Ways to Pursue Excellence*, author Tom Peters makes this point about excellence:

Asked how long it took to achieve excellence, IBM's legendary boss Tom Watson is said to have answered more or less as follows: "A minute. You achieve excellence by promising yourself right now that you'll never again knowingly do anything that's not excellent—regardless of any pressure to do otherwise by any boss or situation."[35]

Strive for excellence in everything your church does. This is especially true when you're partnering with social organizations. On several occasions we have initially been told, "Thanks, but no thanks!" by leaders of social justice organizations that have previously worked with churches only to be left holding the bag with unfinished projects, unpaid bills, and disappointment when a church over-promised and under-delivered.

Here's a good rule of thumb when it comes to anything related to ImpACT—if you're going to do something for ImpACT, do it with excellence:

> Whatever you do, work at it with all your heart, as working for the Lord, not for men, since you know that you will receive an inheritance from the Lord as a reward. It is the Lord Christ you are serving. (Colossians 3:23-24)

"Sometimes I would like to ask God why He allows poverty, suffering, and injustice when He could do something about it."

"Well, why don't you ask Him?"

"Because I'm afraid He would ask me the same question."

—Anonymous

35. Peters, T. *The Little Big Things: 163 Ways to Pursue Excellence*. New York, NY: HarperCollins Publishers 2010, 10.

Simple Acts Change Lives

Every great journey begins with one step. I realize sometimes even that is asking a lot … especially if you're comfortable, well fed, and content just being you. But carrying on as if thousands of people are not dying every day because of lack of food and clean water is unacceptable. We, the Church, are bound by our commitment to Christlikeness to do something. The stakes are too high not to.

Here's how high:

- 16 million children die of hunger each year;[36]
- Every 6 seconds a child dies for lack of pure drinking water;[37]
- 1 billion people do not have access to clean drinking water.[38]

Meeting needs like these takes extraordinary vision, and the rewards are commensurate with the task. It's well worth the effort to overcome life in the ordinary to answer God's call to help and heal the hurting.

God loves every person who will pass into eternity today—the starving mother crying because she has no food for her children, the baby who is dying in her arms, the homeless drug addict who sleeps under a bridge. When you serve such people, they see God's hand at work. By feeding such people, they recognize that God still provides for them. If you give such people a drink of clean water, they feel His presence. When you reach out in tangible acts of kindness, they know God loves them.

I grew up in a poor home and readily imagine how different my idea of the Church would have been if a church would have reached into my family's poverty and given us a hand up every now and then. No one did, though, and it took me years to reconcile that disconnect with the idea that God loves me.

---

36. An End to World Hunger; Hope for the Future, 2010, http://library.thinkquest.org/C002291/high/present/stats.htm.
37. "Water Facts.".
38. Food and Agriculture Organization of the United Nations State of Food Insecurity in the World, 2008.

My early experience is one reason I love doing outreach events directed at kids. Recently, after services ended, we handed each person in our church something we call Changed Life Bags. In every bag were instructions on what to fill the bag with—shoes, socks, underwear, and a toy—and when to bring it back to the church for distribution.

Each bag required our people to make a $25 investment in an elementary kid from a family going through financial hardship. When our people fill these bags, they aren't just stuffing things in a sack, they're showing a little boy or girl that Christ followers care about them and want them to go to school with dignity.

Make a Proposal

Submitting a detailed proposal to a social justice organization is one of the first steps in doing a Second Saturday. You must determine the organization's needs and how you can fit into their plans. Because not every organization will know your parameters, it is good to approach them with a list of ideas of things your church could potentially do.

Admit that Someone Needs You

It's easier to stay comfortable if you convince yourself no one really needs what you have to offer. Or if you think you've got enough trouble of your own to try taking on anyone else's.

At the end of 2008, just after we launched ImpACT, many people in our congregation were hurting. As the economy teetered toward life-support, people were losing their jobs, salaries were being slashed, the housing market was tanking, and people were tightening their purse strings. As I said earlier, it wasn't the best time to ask people to give more to church. Even so, when I pointed out the greater needs that we could meet, people perceived an opportunity to help.

Our plan included getting everyone to buy into the idea of partnering with social justice organizations. We even distributed one-year commitment cards (see Appendix 3) asking for a pledge that would be over and above the tithe, and we encouraged everyone to take part in our Second Saturday events.

"Regular, average, everyday people working together can do something extraordinary and far beyond what we can do individually," I told the congregation. "By working together we can make a difference locally and globally."

The facts—and their own intuition—showed that other people were worse off than most of them. They'd seen neighbors lose their homes and heard of children in far-off countries scrounging for food. If helping these people meant cutting back even more, they were will-ing to do it.

There's no need to twist anyone's arm. When you point out the need and ask for help, people will respond. All of us have something God can use to help others.

Tempt Them Visually

Some of your best advertising will come in the form of flyers and signage on your walls and on your website. These are powerful tools to keep the mission and objective of ImpACT in front of your people. Invest in high-quality, power-ful design and branding.

Empower Agents of Change

When we hear of another person's suffering, it should awaken something within us. It should make us mad, force us to take action. We need to love our fellow man more than we love our politics, prejudices, discussions of theology, and church politics. Love comes first:

"Love the Lord your God with all your heart and with all your soul and with all your mind" (Matthew 22:37).

As a leader of a church, part of your job is to not only get people involved in ImpACT, it's to change the way they think about a broken world. To do that, you need to educate, encourage, and show them how to act like Jesus. To demonstrate what must happen, let me offer an illustration.

Imagine that the people in your church are a bucket. The water in the bucket is your vision for the church. You want that vision to penetrate the hearts and minds of your people, so you begin poking holes in the bucket. Suddenly, *your* vision is running through *your* people. But a problem develops: as it drains, the vision in the bucket begins to run low, and you need a refill…over and over again. As a leader, you need to keep refreshing your vision to keep the bucket filled. All the while, you also have to keep punching holes in the bucket so your vision remains your people's vision.

Everyone needs to be reminded of why they are doing what they are doing and what's at stake. Andy Stanley says casting vision is the job of the leader, and no one cares more about that vision than the leader.[39] Your vision needs to be coursing through the veins of your organization. You have to talk about it, preach it, print it, live by it, and reward people who get it.

Remember, vision leaks through the holes you punch. Life, commitments, and other priorities will distract you from refilling the bucket just as surely as it will clog the holes you make. You'll need to keep punching holes and refilling the bucket so your vision flows constantly through your people.

Show Rather than Tell: *Do* the Right Thing

In Scripture, the Church is compared to a body. Unfortunately, for the last few decades, the mouth of the body of Christ has gotten more exercise than the arms, legs, heart, and brain. We can articulate everything we're against, who we're voting for, who we hate (but we

---

39.   Idea derived from Andy Stanley, *Making Vision Stick*, Grand Rapids, Michigan: Zondervan 2007.

don't call it hate, of course), what rights we're being denied, and what our pseudo-holiness, trendy standards du jour are. But we would be much better served if we just zipped it and served the hurting.

As Rick Warren, pastor of Saddleback Church and author of *The Purpose-Driven Life* points out, "The first Reformation … was about creeds; this one's going to be about our deeds. The first one divided the church; this time it will unify the church."[40] The Bible is explicit about what those deeds are: "Speak up for those who cannot speak for themselves, for the rights of all who are destitute. Speak up and judge fairly; defend the rights of the poor and needy" (Proverbs 31:8-9).

Consistent with genuine love, everything we do to serve and help the impoverished and suffering in our community is done with absolutely no strings attached. We are not interested in bullying or scaring anyone into a relationship with Christ. But if through our actions people feel the love of Christ and are drawn to Him, our investment in the community is well worth it.

If you want to make an ImpACT on the world, make one. It's not rocket science. It doesn't take a highly trained or skilled professional to make an ImpACT. It just takes someone who is willing to make a difference. It doesn't even take a Bible scholar—sometimes not even a Christian. I think it may even be wired into the fabric of life. That's why I appreciate an observation by the ancient Asian guy, Confucius, who said, "To know what is right and not do it is the worst cowardice."[41]

A revolution, a reformation, a sea change begins with one action, one choice, one act of obedience. The world is ready for the Church to be as concerned for the poor and marginalized as Jesus was—to be focused on justice, fairness, and a concern for the needy. Identify needs, and start meeting them.

---

40.   R. Warren, R., & D. Kuo. (n.d.). *Rick Warren's Second Reformation* [Interview]. Retrieved from
Beliefnet website: http://www.beliefnet.com/Faiths/Christianity/2005/10/ Rick-Warrens-Second-Reformation.aspx?p=4
41.   Confucius, K. F.-T. (n.d.). *Englishforums.com* [Quotes]. Retrieved from Englishforums website:
http://www.englishforums.com/English/KungConfuciusRight/llxbr/post.htm

Doing the right thing not only means to do what is correct. It also means do it right where you are, and do it right now. That means you.

CHAPTER 7
IMPLEMENT YOUR LEADERSHIP ABILITIES

I saw a troubling headline recently: "Christianity Is No Longer Americans' Default Faith."[42] Offering support to that notion, a similarly troubling study alleges that only 17 percent of Americans actually attend church.[43]

The church in America is wobbling like a top, losing the battle against the million-and-one other things vying for people's attention. That makes this a tough time—but the best time—for a leader to start a revolution against the things that drag down the church.

I declared North Point Church's revolution on the last Sunday in October 2008. I drew a line in the sand and told my congregation from that moment on we were going to do everything in our power to fight poverty, illiteracy, disease, and spiritual emptiness. I committed us to a fight to give people a voice who don't have one, to use our influence for people who have none.

The question becomes: What does it take for a leader to take on a challenge like this? Perhaps I can give you some ideas.

De-Bug Your Leadership Style

In his book *Killing Cockroaches,* Tony Morgan offers ten easy ways to know you're not a leader:

1. You're waiting on a bigger staff and more money to accomplish your vision;

---

42. Barna Group. (2009, January 12). *Christianity Is No Longer Americans'* Default Faith. Retrieved from The Barna Group website: http://www.barna.org/barna-update/article/12-faithspirituality/ 15-christianity-is-no-longer-americans-default-faith
43. Ibid.

2. You think you need to be in charge in order to have influence;
3. You're content;
4. You tend to foster division instead of generating a helpful dialogue;
5. You think you need to say something to be heard;
6. You find it easier to blame others for your circumstances than to take responsibility for solutions;
7. It's been some time since you said, "I messed up";
8. You're driven by the task instead of the relationships and the vision.
9. Your dreams are so small that people think they can be achieved.
10. No one is following you.[44]

If any of these statements are true of you, it's time to start making some changes. The truth is, no matter how long we've been in leadership, we're probably still coming up short on a point or two. Depending on where you are in your leadership journey and how many of the above statements are true of you, you can consider the rest of this chapter a refresher course on good leadership or Leadership 101. Either way, you'll need to have on your best possible leadership hat when you jump into ImpACT.

Dismiss Criticism and Most Praise

As soon as you start ImpACT, people are going to take notice. Some will love you; others will hate you. In his earthy way, Bob Knight, former coach of the Indiana Hoosiers, observed how he, as a leader viewed his detractors: "When my time on earth has gone, and my activities here are past, I hope they bury me upside down so the critics can kiss my a--."[45]

While I might not recommend saying it quite that way (at least not out loud), Knight's thick-skinned attitude is one that can benefit any leader. Two things to remember: You'll always have supporters, and you'll always have opponents. The truth about you is somewhere in the middle of what these two groups say. So take courage, and don't believe all the bad

44. T. Morgan, *Killing Cockroaches*, Nashville, Tennessee: B&H Publishing Group 2009, 111.
45. *Knight 880: Tribute to Coach Legend* (2007). Retrieved from Knight880.com and RedRaiders.com website: http://www.knight880.com/special/stories/quotes.shtml

things people say about you, your church, your intentions, or the work you're doing. Also keep your feet on the ground, and don't believe all the good things, either.

Say "Thank You" Often

A simple "thank you" can go a long way. Showing appreciation to your staff, volunteers, social justice partner organizations, and even the people your church helps will make a profound and positive impression. Use pulpit time, cards, Facebook, Twitter, your blog, and prayers to regularly thank anyone who helps make ImpACT happen. For sure, thank those who have made an ImpACT pledge (see our Thank-You letters in Appendix 3). At North Point, we also have an annual event specifically to thank our Second Saturday volunteer leaders.

Be sure to thank God, too, for what He accomplishes for you, your church, and community: "Give thanks to the Lord, call on his name; make known among the nations what he has done" (1 Chronicles 16:8).

Break for ImpACT

Having a marathon runner's resolve will get you through the long hauls and rough patches that come with leading a church. You'll also need a sprinter's quickness and power when things get exciting or dicey around your church. When you change your outreach strategy, attack global giants, ask people to give above and beyond their tithe, and focus the church's manpower, finances, and energy toward monthly projects which help the poor and suffering, you are going to need all three: resolve, quickness, and power.

Fortunately, if you follow in the footsteps we've presented in this book, you shouldn't be overcome with fear, stress, or exhaustion, but as with anything worth pursuing, you will have to readjust your church's priorities, make and fulfill new commitments, convince people to get on board with you, and keep the skeptics at bay. Those things take their toll no matter what. That's why you need to take a break every now and then—and not feel guilty about it! When you pull into a rest stop for yourself, you aren't just getting relaxed or finding center; you're also protecting one of the greatest gifts God has given you: your call to do exactly what you're doing.

A few years ago I saw a headline in *The New York Times* praising the movie *Slumdog Millionaire*. The film portrays a guy who discovers what he is truly meant to do and rockets from rags to riches as a result. I had seen it a few days earlier and realized at that moment that everything I was doing in my career—especially ImpACT—was everything I had always wanted and been wired to do. That's a gift only God can give because not only is the work rewarding but so is the satisfaction that comes from battling giants and serving people who are hurting.

No matter how much you love what you're doing, though, you cannot carry ImpACT alone. Choose a few areas where you can serve best, and allow others to step up and run with the program so you don't get burned out.

Part of getting your staff and church to buy into ImpACT is giving them ownership of it. As the campaign grows, you, the leader, will be stretched in every direction. To guard your time and keep the overall vision fresh for everyone, you'll have to delegate authority and focus on the areas of ImpACT where you can have the greatest impact. Allow yourself the "permission" not to participate in every aspect or outreach—and take a break when you know you need it. Be a leader. Work *on* it, not *in* it.

Step Up and Lead Them

Whether you've seen it firsthand or not, churches today are brimming with people who want to make a difference in the world. They want to get involved, to help, and to improve the physical and spiritual lives of those who are poor and suffering. If it's not obvious that an abundance of workers are waiting in the wings, it's because, most of the time, they're missing just one thing: They lack someone to lead them.

They'll step out if only someone will point them in the right direction and empower them to move ahead. Willing-to-help people simply need a leader who is as bent on serving the needy as they are—a leader who rolls up his or her sleeves, goes to the frontlines, and jumps in the trenches to fight your community's global giants. That leader can—and for your church, should—be you.

It may sound really basic, but ImpACT starts with a leader who is willing to fight the bullies. While we all have various personality patterns and different ways God deals with us, we can all have leadership breakthroughs that transform us and our churches. Figure out what breakthroughs you need, and then break through.

Taking a leap forward in leadership is not a science. For me, breakthroughs usually start with frustration and realizing that my life, my church, or my situation needs to go somewhere greater or better than it currently is. But: I often don't know how to move on from where I am. Perhaps you feel that way right now. If you're considering doing ImpACT and want to take your church to another level, here are the practical things I would tell you to do:

- Pray.
- Talk to other leaders you trust, and ask them to shoot straight with you about your ideas and abilities.
- Don't waste time trying to justify where you are stuck, saying things like, "Everything is OK. Most people would be happy to have what I have."
- Prepare to enjoy some sleepless night. Making changes will get you excited around the clock, so relax, and let it toy with your mind. Knowing you can sleep later will probably help you sleep now.
- When a customized vision finally hits you, the fog will lift, and you'll see clearly for the first time in days. That's when it's time to turn the vision into reality.
- Write a rough outline of your vision. Sketch out some details, a timeline, how much it will cost, the changes that will be required, and who needs to be involved.
- Become the champion of your vision. After all the struggle, toil, prayer, and research, it would be hard to talk me out of the vision I've sketched out on paper. You could probably challenge some of the details with me, but I have a mighty good feeling for where God wants me to go with this. Your confidence and commitment will be infectious.

- Lay the rough draft before key leaders. Let them pick it apart and tell you where the blind spots are.
- Take the key leader review as the constructive criticism. Re-draft your vision, and enjoy letting this critical leadership breakthrough generate a realistic, concrete vision.

Be a Good Follower

Before you can lead men and women, you have to be a fully committed follower of God. With the narrative of Jonah, Scripture provides a wild story of what happens to leaders who prefer to go their own way.

Jonah was already a respected prophet in Israel when God presented him with an assignment he just didn't want: Go to Nineveh to preach against that city because it has become so evil. In Jonah's eyes, a trip to Nineveh is a death sentence, and he wants no part of it. He considers God's instruction and promptly hops the first ship out of Joppa going in the other direction.

His escape from God goes as planned until a violent storm arises at sea. Jonah's shipmates wonder who is under such divine censure that God would bring such a severe storm upon them. They cast lots to see who is to blame, and it falls on Jonah. The red-faced prophet explains he is a Hebrew who worships the Lord, the God of heaven but that he had balked at His Divine Master. And this promptly freaks out the sailors. They decide to row back to land, but the storm just grows fiercer. Finally, they determine the only solution is to pitch Jonah into the water:

> Then they cried to the LORD, "O LORD, please do not let us die for taking this man's life. Do not hold us accountable for killing an innocent man, for you, O LORD, have done as you pleased." Then they took Jonah and threw him overboard, and the raging sea grew calm. At this the men greatly feared the LORD, and they offered a sacrifice to the LORD and made vows to him. But the LORD provided a great fish to swallow Jonah, and Jonah was inside the fish three days and three nights. (Jonah 1:14-17)

The belly of the fish ends up being a fine place for Jonah to meditate on his situation. As the figurative light begins to dawn in that dark digestive tract, Jonah realizes, "Those who cling to worthless idols forfeit the grace that could be theirs" (Jonah 2:8). Maybe, just maybe, he shouldn't have been so quick to reject God's leading and forfeit the grace that had been upon him up until then. Jonah saw that it's not risky to surrender everything and obey God, but it is risky not to!

In your case, the real risk may not lie in taking action to fight disease, poverty, illiteracy, and spiritual emptiness, no matter how far it takes you from your comfort zone or how many leadership challenges you face along the way. The real risk lies in not following God there.

Avoid Excuses Like the Plague They Are

Although Jonah didn't outline his excuses for running from God until after he'd visited Nineveh (in Jonah 4:1-3, the prophet "just knew" those doggone Ninevites might actually repent!), they were likely burning in his mind from the beginning. Rationalizing why not to do what you know you should is pretty much an inborn human trait that doesn't need much grooming. Kids are great at it, and adults are, too. As you think about starting ImpACT, even you might be tempted to build a defense against the total surrender that's required, but the Apostle Paul puts to rest every rationalization in the excuse game: "My grace is sufficient for you, for my power is made perfect in weakness" (2 Corinthians 12:9).

Be a Leader Breeder

Delegate.

Delegate.

Delegate.

And did I mention that an indispensable component of good leadership is the ability to wisely and appropriately delegate responsibility to others? To run a long-lasting and effective ImpACT campaign, you have to delegate much of the responsibility to your staff and lay leaders. That means—frightening thought!—you have to trust people.

By delegating, you free yourself to concentrate on the overall campaign and provide opportunities for your staff and lay leaders to grow as leaders. It's the way to do less so you can do more.

Just Say "No" to Mr. Know-it-all

Judas thought he had the whole situation figured out: Jesus is on the wrong track, and Judas develops a plan to set things right. He even reckoned a way to make money in the process. So for 30 coins, this long-time disciple betrays Jesus. Too late, he discovers the limits of his understanding about what was going on. After realizing the gravity of his mistake, guilt sets in, and he goes to the chief priest, elders, and religious leaders to return the cash.

The men want nothing to do with Judas or his money—even they seem to know how cowardly Judas is. The know-it-all disciple suddenly knows nothing but overwhelming guilt and shame. He flings the money into the temple, runs away, and hangs himself.

Now the religious leaders pick up the know-it-all mantle: "The chief priests picked up the coins and said, 'It is against the law to put this into the treasury, since it is blood money'" (Matthew 27:6). It's appalling that the "church" leaders of that day had no problem killing Jesus but didn't want to violate a minor point of their law by putting blood money into the treasury.

Now the religious leaders pick up the know-it-all mantle: "The chief priests picked up the coins and said, 'It is against the law to put this into the treasury, since it is blood money'" (Matthew 27:6). It's appalling that the "church" leaders of that day had no problem killing Jesus but didn't want to violate a minor point of their law by putting blood money into the treasury.

Key Leadership Positions for ImpACT

Here are the key leaders we use at North Point. You can use whatever titles you choose, but these show the essential functions:

Resource Director – Heads up the process; executes day of the event; stamps his approval on projects.

2nd Saturday Director – reports to Resource Director, plans and executes events, contacts partners, works with them on projects, contacts leaders for day of event, manages in-house projects for events as well as ImpACT promotions. (Changed Life Bags, mailers, emails to volunteers, reminders to volunteers, data entry, supply ordering, etc.); plans event and execution; works with event leaders day of.

2nd Saturday Coordinator – Supports 2nd Saturday Director, can be second contact for partners, manages projects (Changed Life Bags, mailers, emails to volunteers, reminders to volunteers, data entry, supply ordering, etc.).

Awesome Leaders Day Of – They help execute day of the event; head up volunteers for different areas and different projects; leaders do not DO day of, they manage/direct.

Facilities Director – You would most likely need a facility/maintenance person involved to help with work projects.

Are you ever guilty of thinking you know more than you really do? Are you or your church ever so ignorant and clueless that you would "strain out a gnat and swallow a camel"?

I submit that when a church and its leaders waste energy arguing about the evils of Harry Potter or the latest sitcom on NBC instead of doing something about the fact that every 3.6 seconds someone dies of hunger, they aren't seeing the forest for the trees. When Christian organizations sue other Christian organizations and dismiss 1 Corinthians 6 which says not to take other followers of Christ to court, they're making serious missteps that hurt the kingdom of God. When you spend your influence on things that make you bigger but not better, you're wasting God's resources.

When you fail to acknowledge that only God knows it all and in love wants to break you and make you like Him, it's impossible for ImpACT to take hold. There is too much of you and not enough of God for ImpACT to do its thing. Just in case you wonder whether or not you've got things figured out, here's the answer: You don't.

Get Ready for a Brawl

You'd think reaching into your community with God's grace and mercy would make everyone happy, but oddly enough, it doesn't. In fact, you'll likely face some of the greatest spiritual, financial, and logistical challenges of your ministry career. Which is why you need to be prepared for some fights. Exercise diplomacy first, of course, but don't back down from the conflicts that will inevitably arise at some point.

One of the best ways to prepare for the fights to come is on your knees, and sometimes the very best combat technique is simply to be nice to your opponents. Prayer will grant you discernment about how to fight.

We've had some surprising battles thrust in our faces, but I can tell you that "nice" does often win the day. One organization we approached about letting us partner with them refused our offer. Because of our commitment not to re-invent the wheel, their position blocked our advance against the giants. In the past, the organization explained, they had been burned by churches who over-promised and under-delivered. We realized we would have to earn their trust, so we "bought them off." Instead of giving them our service, we gave them our money—a nice check with no strings attached—and we gained their trust. They saw we were serious, and the next year we again asked if we could do a community project with them. The second time, they could hardly say "Yes" fast enough!

Sometimes when you brawl, the first step is to take the fall. After that, you'll have others picking you up to help them fight.

Set the Standard

If you're going to ask your congregation to give above and beyond their tithe to finance ImpACT, you, as the leader, need to set the standard of giving. Each year, I give above my tithe for ImpACT. I'm committed to making a difference and know I must set the pace when it comes to sacrifice and giving. If you want your congregation to buy into your vision for ImpACT, you have to buy into it more than anyone else, and that begins with cracking open your wallet and going public with your commitment.

Be a Risk Taker

It's been said that when you live, you risk dying. So what are we to do? Every day we run the ultimate risk (dying), whether it's by driving to the store or walking across the street. We also take less physical risks like putting our feelings on the line by telling someone we love them. So yes, you are a risk taker, whether you mean to be or not.

If you've tended to be risk-averse, then starting ImpACT is a great time to accept risk as a natural part of life. ImpACT requires you to take risks. You risk disappointing people who would rather keep things the way they are. You even risk rejection by those you want to help (like the organization that wouldn't let us help them). It's scary to venture into the unknown, but as with any high-yield investment, the rewards outweigh the risks.

In his book, *The Disney Way,* elder statesman of modern management Peter Drucker writes, "When you see a successful business, someone once made a courageous decision."[46] Those who have prospered despite obstacles in the path rely on an inner compass to steer their course: deeply held values that have crystallized and led them to achieve tangible results. Walt Disney, the great storyteller and innovator, had just such a compass that even now, years after his death, defines his one-of-a-kind empire. Disney's four steps were simple:

---

46.   In B. Capodagli & L. Jackson, *The Disney Way*, McGraw-Hill 2007, xi.

1. Dream beyond the boundaries of today.
2. Believe in sound values.
3. Dare to make a difference.
4. And then just go out and do it: Dream, Believe, Dare, Do.[47]

Notice that none of the steps say, "Avoid risks." They're inherent in any big dream.

Be Happy

For some people, this leadership trait will come more naturally than for others. But no matter what your temperament, being happy doesn't just happen to you. It is a choice.

If you're a happy person, studies suggest you will have a stronger immune system, be a more productive worker, and live longer than someone who isn't happy. So what makes people happy? It's not money, intelligence, the shape of your body, security, attractiveness, success, or even good health. According to the *The Journal of Happiness Studies,* the factor that distinguishes consistently happier people from less happy people is the presence of rich, deep, joy-producing, life-changing, meaningful relationships with other human beings!

A sure-fire way to develop these happiness-building relationships is through working alongside people while serving others. So guess what ImpACT offers? A stellar opportunity for you, and anyone in your church who gets involved, to be happy. Show me someone who gives consistently of his or her time to the benefit of others, and I'll show you a happy person. And I'll show you an even happier person when that is done side-by-side with others. When people live outside themselves and adopt a "we" rather than "me" existence, life-changing things happen.

A shadow effect of individual happiness is that it helps your church put its best foot forward. As you and your people become a happy, integral part of the community, people outside the church take note.

---

47.   Ibid.

Cut 'em Loose

Not all of the people you trust with responsibility will live up to your expectations, and unfortunately, sometimes you just can't know that until you've tried and they've failed. When that happens, you'll have to part ways with an ImpACT leader who may otherwise end up doing more harm than good. Such times are never easy, but good leaders must make difficult decisions for the betterment of ImpACT, the church, and the community, even if it puts an individual participant through a tough experience.

There are several reasons why one of your leaders might need to be let go or at least cautioned and coached. Here are three reasons I've had to face:

(1) The leader has lost commitment to the vision. As bad as it sounds, this is not the end of the world. Sometimes a lack of commitment to the church's vision can be corrected. If so, you might consider giving the leader a chance to get on board with your vision. But if the problem persists, you'll need an exit strategy that is good for everyone involved and protects the ministry of ImpACT and preserves the unity of your church.

(2) The leader once had the ability and skill to serve, but ImpACT has outgrown the leader's capabilities. The truth is, it takes a very different set of skills to serve as a leader in ImpACT when it first starts than when it is reaching thousands of people during a Second Saturday event. Dismissing a good person with limited leadership ability is one of the hardest conversations you'll have. You want to honor the good intentions of the leader, but your top priority is to do whatever is best for the growth of ImpACT and your church.

 Look for other, better-fitting leadership roles within ImpACT for the leader in question. If there are none, shoot straight with the person anyway, and offer him or her a non-leadership role.

(3) The leader has ignored coaching about his or her attitude or has begun to cause division. This is the most difficult situation to address. Sometimes just a

kick in the pants can get a person's attention so everyone can get back on the same page. But if the sour apple has to go, it has to go.

One thing I have learned about any of these situations is to deal with them immediately! The longer you wait, the bigger the problem will become. Seek healing and restoration with the leader, of course, but keep your focus on the primary goal of maintaining the health of ImpACT and your church. The responsibility rests with you. Your staff, volunteers, and social justice partners are relying on you to do what's best.

Young Leaders Need a Role, Too

Researchers have found that twenty-somethings don't like attending traditional worship services; they shy away from labels and are drawn to smaller more intimate settings. Even so, they demonstrate an overwhelming belief in God and an interest in all things spiritual that relate to their lives and world.[48]

I'd also add that twenty-somethings don't mind being challenged, asked to get their hands dirty, and given tasks to do that can make a difference in their community and the world. At North Point Church, we engage our twenty-somethings by trusting them to participate and lead ImpACT.

No matter who your leaders are, each one must have an area where they not only excel, but they also get people to serve your guests with the best customer service ever experienced.

---

48. Catalystspace.com, November 2006.

Be a Life-long Student

Every day the world is changing, Christian culture is shifting, and leadership trends are emerging. To stay abreast of those changes, you need to read books and periodicals about the world around you and that help you make ImpACT the most relevant it can be.

Once you've finished this book, here are several more you need to read as soon as possible:

- *unChristian: What a New Generation Really Thinks about Christianity...and Why It Matters* by David Kinnaman and Gabe Lyons;
- *It: How Churches and Leaders Can Get It and Keep It,* by Craig Groeschel;
- *Descending into Greatness* by Bill Hybels;
- *Connecting* by Larry Crab;
- *The Hole in Our Gospel* by Richard Stearns.

These are just a few of my favorites, but you get the point. Read, stay informed, and influence your world.

Surround Yourself with People Who Won't Tell You Lies

People want to make a difference in the world, and your job is to give them an opportunity to do it. If you do your job well, you'll connect with people, tap into their consciences, inspire them to compassion, and convince them that helping people is not only biblical, it's good for the individual, church, and community. Do that, and you'll have a following of faithful people—but there's a problem with their faithfulness. People who follow you because you've inspired and encouraged them to be their best selves will rarely challenge you. On the surface, that may sound pretty nice, but the truth is, every leader needs someone or some people who will tell them when they're off base.

One reason our nation's economy was brought to its knees was the lack of honesty among people managing the mortgage banking business. Everyone wanted to hear only the good news. Bad news was shuffled under the table. Sorry! Good news can make you feel nice, but it doesn't always serve you well in the long run. Bad news can be an alarm to protect you from serious problems.

To get the most out of ImpACT, you need people who will tell you how things really are around you, assess you honestly, and help keep you on the straight and narrow. Surround yourself with people who won't tell you lies.

> **"Tell me and I'll forget, show me and I may remember, involve me and I'll understand."** —Chinese proverb

Ask the Right (and Tough) Questions

A corollary to surrounding yourself with people who will be honest with you is to always be ready to ask the questions that need to be asked, no matter how difficult the implications may be to face. It starts with the type of question raised at the beginning of the first chapter: Whatever the tragedy—a sudden cataclysm like the earthquake in Haiti or the sinister, creeping poverty in our own communities—don't ask, "Where is God?" Ask, "Where are we in this crisis, and what are we going to do to help?"

Here are some more questions to have ready for the right time:

- What will you do to right the wrongs?
- How can you be the one who gives someone else hope?
- Where should we focus our church's time, finances, and energy to make the biggest difference possible?
- What have we been missing?

By extending the love of Christ in times of need, you will change this world for the better. But don't waste your time looking for God in the midst of despair. Take Him to where He is needed most.

Character, Chemistry, and Competency Are Crucial

At a Willow Creek Leadership Summit, I once heard Bill Hybels speak on the critical factors for strong leadership. He described "three C's" for good leaders—character, chemistry, and competency—and you'll want to keep these in mind when looking for people to lead an area of ImpACT.

Sometimes the most obvious candidate for a role in ImpACT is exactly the wrong person. Perhaps it's someone you know will quickly say "yes" to a request for help, but the person's skill set or personality may not be what you need. Hold out for the right choice to show up.

You'll also need to watch out for those who can naturally hit homeruns for you, but who, in the process cause disunity, imbalance, offense, or dissension. That's too steep of a price to pay. You do not want to spend your time managing the problems that the "wrong" person causes.

You can avoid the wrong person issue by doing some homework before turning over the reins to a potential ImpACT leader. Check out their three C's:

- Character—Is the person you're considering for leadership a person of good character?
- Chemistry—Is he or she easy to work with?
- Competency—Does the individual have the skills to carry out the job?

To supplement your own judgment, have other trusted leaders spend a little time with those you are considering for specific roles, and evaluate them based on the three C's.

You Need Somebody to Lean On

Solid, spiritual friendships are key to your wellbeing and the success of ImpACT in your church and community. A friend to lean on is one who:

- You can call at any time;
- Will root for you;
- Holds you accountable;
- Will challenge you;
- Disciples you;
- Prays with and for you;
- Loves you despite your shortcomings;
- Makes time for you.

Spiritual friendships are meaningful. God created us in His image. He created us to have a capacity and need for connectedness with others. "The Lord God said, 'It is not good for the man to be alone. I will make a helper suitable for him'" (Genesis 2:18).

Even not-specifically-Christian sociological research bears this out. According to Robert Putnam in his book *Bowling Alone:*

> The single most common finding from a half-century's research on life satisfaction not only from the U.S., but from around the world, is that happiness is best predicted by the depth of one's social connections.[49]

As a leader, you need friends who will stand by you. Having a strong network of people you can depend on will ensure your church has the most ImpACT it can. Respond true or false to the following statements to help you determine if you need to make some more friends:

- The only friends on your Facebook page are your spouse and children.
- The only person in your community outside your family and church who knows your first name is the barista at Starbucks.

---

49.   Robert D. Putnam, *Bowling Alone: the Collapse and Revival of American Community*, New York: Simon & Schuster 2000, 332.

- You think your city's chamber of commerce is a bank.
- You like people … you just can't stand to be around them.

If you answered true to any of the statements above, you need to branch out and start making some new friends. It will open doors of opportunity for your church to meet needs and give people hope.

CHAPTER 8

IMPOSE THE RIGHT RULES

Every healthy organization should have well-written vision, mission, and purpose statements, right? That's certainly what we've been taught to think, anyway. But I have to confess that at some point in the not-too-distant past, I began to lose track of the distinctions between vision, mission, and purpose. And then it hit me: If I don't know the difference between our mission statement and our vision statement, our people certainly can't know the difference! That's the day I decided to keep it simple.

I guess I'm in good company in thinking that way, too. Management expert Peter Drucker says your main thing (mission statement, I think) should be so simple it should be able to fit on the front of a T-shirt.[50]

When a leader is casting vision, the goal is to communicate the main thing. Call it vision, mission, purpose, or your latest Facebook post, but people better be able to read it and say, "I know the main thing." In fact, simply calling it your Main Thing may not be a bad idea.

For North Point Church, I realized we are all about "changed lives." Having said that, I can explain a hundred different ways we strategically plan to change lives (and I will tell you some of them in this chapter), but to make those the up-front statements would eliminate clarity and lead us nowhere. When communicating what your church or organization is all about, keep it simple.

So, first figure out your main thing. What is it, and how can you say it simply? If you don't know, or it takes you some time to explain it, no one else knows your main thing, either. For

---

50.   Drucker, P. *Creating an effective Mission Statement* (June 2006). Retrieved from http://www.brs-inc.com/news002.html

instance, ImpACT is a complicated program, but we explain the purpose by saying simply that we're "fighting four global giants."

Once you know your main thing, then there are some other rules of the road which will help you accomplish whatever the main thing is. I've sorted through more possibilities than I can count but have distilled in the remainder of this chapter some of the rules, ideas, and attitudes that have been most helpful at North Point. Hopefully, they'll help you accomplish your main thing, too.

Money Breaks Down Walls

Money can be a very effective sledgehammer. It has the power to break down most any wall that keeps your church from helping in the community. When I came up with the ImpACT idea, I decided to direct our missions funds to local and international social justice organizations which were making a difference battling the four giants.

Each year I deliver a three- or four-week sermon series on ImpACT and ask everyone to make a financial pledge. It's better if everyone buys into ImpACT—no matter how much or little they can give—than to have just a few deep pockets bankroll the deal. I ask for 100 percent participation.

Throughout the year, we also ask the congregation to buy bikes, school supplies, clothing, and toys for local kids. When a family buys a bike or a toy for our Christmas outreach, they feel a special sense of ownership (literally and figuratively) in the program. To make ImpACT successful, you must continually remind your people that it's not just about serving, it's about giving as well.

The Power of an ImpACT Pledge

A 12-month ImpACT pledge is a great sacrifice for most families, but it's also an excellent opportunity for people to make an investment in the lives of others that pays eternal dividends. For North Point Church, here's what ImpACT pledges accomplish:

- Help fund the program for a year;
- Start a multi-church campus strategy to multiply our influence;
- Help those who are homeless, illiterate, hungry, fighting life-threatening diseases, or who have addictions and give them influence in solving their problems;
- Mitigate spiritual emptiness on college campuses, in communities, across the nation, and overseas for those who have not experienced life change through Jesus Christ;
- Allow us to partner with social justice organizations;
- Assist the impoverished with clothing, food, and shelter;
- Care for the sick and diseased with a variety of medical services;
- Teach literacy.

Give More than Money

Like I said, ImpACT is about giving both time and money. It's holistic, and the people of your church need to own it.

Maybe it's because the United States is so insulated. Maybe it's because the average American has so many luxuries. Maybe it's because we've been building our personal empires for so long. Maybe it's just because we've become apathetic. I don't know why, but many Americans are willing to give money to help others out—but not many will actually roll up their sleeves, jump in the trenches, and join the fight.

To give money is one part of the ImpACT commitment. Giving time is the other essential component. You need to implore your people to give both. The reason some people don't feel compelled to give one or the other is that their leader lacks a passionate vision for why both are required.

With ImpACT you need to be bold, aggressive and excited about the outreaches and the work your church is doing. When you are, people will buy what you're selling. They'll open their wallets and hearts. You cannot reach the poor and suffering without your people buying in with their time as well as their money.

Build Bridges, Not Walls

To be efficient and effective, your church will need to connect with other churches, agencies, and organizations so you have opportunity to build bridges with those who are poor and suffering.

In Luke 14, Jesus tells the parable of a great banquet. A wealthy man planned a gala event and invited many acquaintances of his social class or higher, but one by one each guest rejected his invitation. In the culture of that day, there were very few legitimate excuses for missing such a banquet. The clear implication is that the invitees were deliberately attempting to humiliate the man, trying to ridicule him in an attempt to stop the banquet. Enraged, the man has his servants go into the "streets and alleys of the town and bring in the poor, the crippled, the blind and the lame" (Luke 14:21).

As always, Jesus was not just telling an entertaining story, he was making a point. This one was directed at the religious leaders of the day who had become exclusive. They liked building insurmountable walls between themselves and regular people, but Jesus didn't think much of their approach. At His banquet, He intends to fill the seats. He doesn't just want His followers building kingdoms that only serve other followers. He wants to reach "outsiders" and bring them into the fold. He wants to build bridges. The parable demonstrates how to reach the unchurched and how to build a church people will want to come to: "Go out to the roads and country lanes and make them come in, so that my house will be full" (Luke 14:23).

Press On

German speed skater, Patrick Beckert, blew his chance to compete in the 2010 Winter Olympics. As the fourth alternate, it was extremely unlikely he would get called up to race, but when two-time gold medalist Enrico Fabris of Italy withdrew from the race one hour before it was to begin, officials attempted to reach the first three alternates, but none were available. The Germans tried desperately to find Beckert, but his cell phone was turned off. Seventeen minutes before the race, Beckert finally checked in, but it was too late.

Though his chances of getting to race were slim, Beckert should have been at the oval, just in case. If you play it smart, sometimes you can arrange to be "in the right place at the right time." You never know what doors God will open in the eleventh hour.

The same is true with ImpACT. Sometimes, even when your intentions are pure, you come up against fierce resistance that threatens to derail your plans, but don't give up. Be ready to serve your community. Be available! Also, plan your ImpACT, but be open to needs that arise without warning. Unexpected crises will present opportunities to help, such as the 2011 tornado that devastated Joplin, Missouri, just 70 miles from North Point Church.

Live Below Your Means

Since you'll be asking your people to give sacrificially as part of ImpACT, you'll want to offer encouragement and guidance about how they can do what you say. Long ago, I learned a simple plan to manage personal finances, and it has kept me out of debt, helped me save money, and kept my giving on track:

> For every $10 you earn, give $1 to the church as a tithe. Also, save $1, and use the remaining $8 to live on. Giving and saving this way forces people to live beneath their means in a healthy way. It will also prepare them to make above-and-beyond contributions to meaningful work such as ImpACT.

By teaching your church godly finances and how it directly correlates with ImpACT, you will not only help your people live more solid financial lives, you'll be furthering your ImpACT as well.

Bottom line

Here is a simple equation: Spend Less + Save More = Ability to Give More to Those in Need. Simple, but not easy to live up to. Consider the following facts:

- $15,519 = average credit card debt per household in the United States[51]
- $2.44 trillion = total U.S. consumer debt[52]
- $392 = average amount Americans save each year.[53]

Save Arm Wrestling for the Playground

Staff, volunteers, partners, and recipients are the key players in your ImpACT campaign. One of the best ways to treat them with respect and let them know you value them is never to twist arms to enlist their help. If you have to twist a person's arm, he or she is not ready to take part in what you're doing. That principle applies to everything from partnering with your church to accepting Christ as Savior. Bullying people into a relationship with your church or with Jesus or begging someone to take part in ImpACT are set-ups for failure.

Let time and the Holy Spirit do their work. Be patient. Be receptive. And let people know they're a piece of the puzzle you believe God has called you to assemble. For some people, their part of the puzzle might be making a commitment to Christ. For others, it might be cleaning toilets at an outreach.

Whatever the situation, you don't have to twist people's arms to get results. Through your acts of kindness and service, people will be drawn to Christ, and servants will rise up to take on responsibilities so others can have a better life and the opportunity to know Jesus.

---

51. "Making Dollars and Cents of Credit Card Balance Transfer Offers," September 2010, http://www.smartbalancetransfers.com/dollars-credit-card-balance-transfer-offers/.

52. Morgenson, Gretchen, "The Debt Trap–Given a Shovel, Americans Dig Deeper Into Debt," The New York Times, July 2008, accessed August 2010, http://www.nytimes.com/2008/07/20/business/20debt.html?pagewanted=3#.

53. Ibid.

Shower Them with Kindness

When North Point partners with local social justice organizations, we do it with no strings attached. Absolutely none. We don't make them listen to sermons, read tracts, or drink our Kool-Aid®. We simply have open hands and hearts to help.

Even so, some organizations have a hard time trusting churches. When that's the case, we take it slow, and let the organization take the lead. Most times, we'll make a financial contribution but not necessarily join them in a project during a Second Saturday event.

Money changes people's perspective. By giving a gift up front, it sets the table for future partnering. It's the slow road to friendship, but one that ultimately makes the relationship stronger. When they see we really mean no strings attached, they are usually open to partnering with us on a project as our relationship grows. If you've never tried it, you'll be astounded at the goodwill your church begins to have in your community when you give first and give freely.

Become a Self-feeder and Teach It to Your People

Part of ImpACT takes place out of sight—in the realm of personal growth. I call it being a self-feeder. You develop the ability to nurture your own spiritual life and learn what you need to know in order to become effective in touching your community. Here's the recipe for self-feeding:

- Read your Bible and pray regularly;
- Surround yourself with accountability partners who hold your feet to the fire when you screw up;
- Serve willingly and without complaining in your church;
- Pour your life into other people's lives;
- Tithe 10 percent of your income regularly;
- Buy into and support the ImpACT vision;
- Never say, "Feed me, feed me!" because you feed yourself.

Stay Broken

Don't think because you are a follower of Christ, you're superior to those who aren't. That's been a hallmark of Christians for far too long. Instead, continue to have a broken heart and spirit before God so He can continue to trust you with His influence. Recognize that you never get over your need for God. You always "are weak, but He is strong."

Embrace the Big Guys

In 2010, North Point teamed up with Convoy of Hope to help feed tens of thousands of children and respond to the earthquake in Haiti. We also participated in One Prayer, which saw thousands of churches join together to pray, fast, and serve their communities.

Teaming up with international organizations and partnering with national movements suddenly transforms your church into a major league player in the war on the global giants. They may seem big, but they're always on the look-out for help. Often, the bigger the organization, the more it aspires to do, which means the more it needs your help. Be there for them!

The Work of "One Prayer"

One Prayer began in 2008 to explore the question: We pray to Jesus asking Him to answer our prayers—what if we became the answer to His? In John 17:20-24, He prayed that we would be one, and One Prayer is an opportunity to see what can be accomplished when the Church works together. One Prayer shares training and resources among the participating churches in order to reach the unreached (see http://2010.oneprayer.com/). In just three years, more than 2,000 churches have participated in this prayer ministry with the result that 2,700 churches have been planted in China, Cambodia, India, and Sudan (see http://swerve.lifechurch.tv/category/one-prayer/).

Have Laser Focus

Undertaking a Second Saturday outreach requires pinpoint focus. At any given outreach event, address one problem. Don't try to solve every social ill in your community. Isolate one concern or one organization, and go after it with all you've got. If you aren't focused solely on your global giants, rather than being laser-powered your effectiveness will be reduced to a flashlight with low batteries. Any light you shine on the problem will make only marginal change.

Make It Easy to Help

If you want ImpACT to succeed, you have to be over-the-top organized. When 30—or 300—volunteers show up to serve at a Saturday morning outreach, it's your job to make sure they feel like it was worth it from the minute they arrive until the minute they leave. If you don't, you probably won't see them at the next month's event.

Most of your volunteers are busy with family, career, school, hobbies, and other commitments. If they get to your outreach and have to figure out what you want them to do, be prepared for frustration and disenchantment. You can avoid that by being well prepared. The most basic principle is to stay on schedule. If volunteers see that you respect their time commitment, you'll likely have all the regular help you need.

Have a Volunteers' To-do List at Every Second Saturday Event

Imparting detailed instructions to your volunteer leaders on the day of your Second Saturday event is imperative and will help everything run smoothly (see Appendix 4 for more about Second Saturday events and planning materials).

Keep Your Promises

For our Second Saturday outreaches, we promise our volunteers we will start at 8:00 and finish by noon. We do everything in our power to stick with that time frame, and it's amazing what we can pack into those four hours.

To repaint, clean, and refurbish an entire school in half a day takes an unbelievable amount of organization and planning. But we believe in the concept of pay me now or pay me later. One way or another, the work of managing has to happen, or nothing productive will take place. By planning and being prepared to serve, no time is wasted, volunteers are kept busy doing meaningful work, and the partners we help see our effectiveness and efficiency.

Keeping the promise of only four hours of work tells our volunteers we value and appreciate their time enough to have all the kinks worked out before they arrive. That increases the likelihood they will come back the following month.

Leave it better than you found it

If you took shop class in junior high school, you'll recall being told to leave the shop better than you found it. That meant making sure everything was cleaned and put away properly. The same is true with your event.

Make sure the project is complete, clean, and done with excellence. There is nothing worse for your church's reputation with other organizations than sloppy work, over-promising and under-delivering, or leaving the site worse than when you arrived.

Give People Something to Talk About

At North Point Church, we use personal stories, multimedia, popular and sacred music, drama, and many other art forms to communicate the timeless truths of God's love each and every week. Many times, because of ImpACT, unchurched people visit us the Sunday after a Second Saturday event. Our goal is to make it easy and non-threatening for such visitors to come our church, check things out, and explore the claims of Christ without being weirded out or pressured into a decision they won't stick with.

Sometimes we take hits for doing church the way we do it. Once we did a sermon series entitled "Girls Gone Wild, Bible Style." People who had never considered coming to church flocked to us after we sent out thousands of mailers advertising the series. Dozens of people who had never before darkened a church doorway committed their lives to Christ during the series. It was amazing to see so many people from myriad backgrounds come to church, be captivated by the message, and commit their lives to Jesus Christ. We took some flack and gave people something to talk about, but dozens of people experienced life change… well worth the hits we took.

Did I mention that in the process of making the right rules, you have to break a few, too? Yet sometimes that's exactly what's required to get people truly passionate about what you're doing.

CHAPTER 9

IMPASSION YOUR PEOPLE

Ron, a former Marine, did not grow up in church and never considered giving it a chance because he didn't feel like "religion" was for him. If asked why he never went to church, he would usually tell people he thought Christians were odd and judgmental. But when he heard that North Point Church was performing songs by The Beatles for a Christmas series dubbed "Revolution" he decided to check us out.

Ron liked the music well enough, but he still wasn't convinced we were for real. He sat silently waiting for us to blow it, to do something that would reaffirm all the reasons he had accumulated not to give church or Jesus a place in his life. Just as he was sure we couldn't keep up the "masquerade," I held up a plastic bag with a kid's name on it and asked everyone in the congregation to pick one up after the service. I told each person to fill it with a new toy and a winter coat so we could give it to impoverished kids in our community for Christmas.

"It was cool," Ron told me later. "I saw immediate action. North Point Church was being human and not religious."

Our action resonated with Ron and quickly overcame his cynicism.

"They focused on doing good," he says, "and that spoke louder than anything they could have preached."

Ron is a great example of how the ImpACT vision is kindled in people. Yet igniting the spark is just the first step in getting your congregation fired up. Your long term success with the program rests in the degree to which the people involved become passionate about what they're doing. In this chapter, as you prepare for your own ImpACT, I'll leave you with a handful or two of straightforward ways you can energize people for the work ahead.

A Me Church or a Re-Church?

After much consideration, I've decided that— regardless of denomination, size, geographic location, member demographics, or doctrinal focus—there are really only two different kinds of churches. You can be either a Me Church or a Re-Church, where "Re" stands for "Reach." Let me explain the difference by walking you through a series of questions you can use to find out which kind yours is.

The book *Simply Strategic Growth* notes that if you're a "Me Church" your people will ask questions such as:

- What if the church gets too big?
- What is the church doing for me?
- How can we avoid change, so people don't feel uncomfortable?
- How do we get the people who left our church to come back?
- When are we going to get to the meat?
- Why aren't we digging deeper?[54]

On the other hand, if you're a "Reach Church" your people will ask questions such as:

- How can we include more people?
- What is the church doing for those who need us most?
- What could we do differently to reach people in our community who are not connected to God?
- How do we get new people to attend our services?
- How do we make the Bible easier to understand and apply to people's lives?

See the difference? Guess which one I prefer?

---

54.   Tim Stevens, Tony Morgan, and Ed Young, *Simply Strategic Growth: Attracting a Crowd to Your Church,* Loveland, CO: Group Publishing 2005, 39-40.

While philosophically I lean more towards being a Reach Church, I readily admit that a healthy church needs to develop a comfortable blend of the two. Jesus said to make disciples. So we do. But for me that also means, as we reach people, we take them on a journey to become fully devoted Christ followers. We are not only going to reach people, we are going to help them grow spiritually by serving others, by teaching them to read their Bibles, by attending church, praying, joining community groups, and taking part in our monthly outreaches to change the world.

Big-idea Things Attract Big-idea People

One of our unwritten rules is to let people step up and shine. Dozens of leaders have identified themselves to us during our monthly outreaches by stepping up with passion, innovation, and determination. We've found that big-idea people are drawn to big-idea things, and ImpACT is one of the biggest-idea things going.

If you provide a clear vision and a detailed plan of what you want people to do, your big-idea people will rise to the top, and the passion they develop will help energize others on your team. What's more, there's a corollary to this big-idea people concept that applies to the organizations you work with: Big people are attracted to big things; small people are attracted to small things—and small people cause problems.

Big Dreams Make Big Partners Even Better

When partnering with a local social justice organization, you may find that one of the greatest hurdles is helping them identify the best way you and your army of volunteers can help. At North Point, we realized that many organizations initially had no concept of what it meant that our 300 volunteers could do $30,000 worth of work for them in just four hours on a Saturday morning.

We regularly dreamed big about what we could accomplish because we knew what was possible. Usually, we had to be the dream leaders for the partner organizations. They weren't used to assistance on the scale we could provide, but imparting that vision is not always an easy task. We encourage our partners to dream big dreams—and we show them how it's done.

We want partners to grasp the scope of what we can do and to fully believe there are no strings attached. If we do those two things, they will get excited at the prospect of our partnership (see Partnership Letter in Appendix 4).

Sometimes, for starters, it requires an on-site visit to their location and an evaluation of their facilities and needs by one of our leaders. Often in the initial consultation visit, the partner will start dreaming the big dreams they need in order to take complete advantage of what ImpACT has to offer.

Launch with a Blast

When you announce ImpACT to your church, you need to do it in high style. Your enthusiasm and passion (or lack of it) will determine whether your launch is a hit or a dud. You can increase the blast factor by teasing your people with pre-launch announcements explaining that something great is going to take place on your chosen date (see several bulletin insert series in Appendix 3). When launch day arrives, make it as fun and memorable as possible while conveying the desperate needs you intend to meet in your community.

Work the Media

Whether you feel like it or not, what you'll be doing in ImpACT is news. How come? Because it's unusual for a church to be giving away bikes, restoring public schools, putting new bedding in every dorm of the Boys & Girls Town, and giving away thousands of toys at Christmas. With almost every major Second Saturday event we hold, the media cover what we're doing. They need news content, and our action in the community fills that need—big time.

Press releases (see Appendix 4), Tweets, blogs, Facebook posts, and calls to action from the pulpit can mean the difference between whether or not volunteers show up, organizations get on board with your church, and people come to your event to get help. Use every medium you can to inform your church and community of your ImpACT event. Be creative, consistent, and compelling. Working the media will not only get coverage for your events, it will encourage your people along the way and inspire other churches to do something to help your community as well.

Your church will feel like it is part of something big.

Just Add Sugar

If ImpACT isn't fun and exciting for you, your staff, and volunteers, it won't last. I once saw a kid wearing a T-shirt that read: Good kid … just add sugar. As the leader, you need to find out what ingredient(s) will make ImpACT fun and exciting for the folks in your church.

For North Point, the T-shirt would read: Good ImpACT … just add simplicity. By casting vision, delegating responsibilities, planning and being organized, we keep it simple; we keep it fun.

Let Your Reputation Make You Rich (in Good Works)

Many wealthy people get that way because they have learned how to make money when they aren't working. The same principle applies to your expanding the reach of your church if you treat your reputation as the precious currency it is.

A good reputation in the community when you're doing ImpACT will earn you tremendous dividends. Establishing a solid standing in your area isn't hard, but it is crucial. Here are a few basics which will set you on the path to a great reputation and the rewards that deliver:

- Always finish a task you've promised to complete;
- Make a priority of clear communication with everyone involved;
- Treat people the way you want to be treated;
- Strive for excellence;
- Share any praise or accolades you receive.

Your credibility is everything—especially with the social justice organizations you partner with to make your community better. Together, you will invest prodigious amounts time and resources in the relationship, and the organization will extend generous amounts of trust to your church. When you guard that trust, you'll protect your credibility and build your reputation.

It would be a shame to blow everything because of poor judgment, miscommunication, not following through on your project, or over-promising and under-delivering. So don't. And make sure no one on your team does.

Building credibility and trust with social justice organizations can take time. So finish what you start. Don't overstep your boundaries. And give and serve with no strings attached.

Embrace Unresolved Tension

Tension. We think of it as being a bad thing. And it's true that unresolved tension between people can be painful, heart wrenching, and destructive over time, but it can also be a stimulus to propel us to greater things.

Art, music, poetry, scientific breakthroughs, relationships, countries, and even churches grow out of creative use of tension—usually the tension that something's not quite right combined with a vision that the problem can be resolved. Without tension and the accompanying feelings of discontent, the world would be missing many blessings. Unresolved tension once convinced me to leave a great position at a large church to start a congregation that un-churched people would love and find relevant.

It's scary to imagine what the world would be like if there were no struggles within our hearts and minds. Perhaps as never before, unresolved tension is becoming a positive force in our churches. Entire generations of people who are captivated by Jesus are beginning to rebel against the petty politics and traditions that exist in many congregations. It fuels a passion to find ways to be an example of Christ to a dying world, and it's a passion you want to tap into.

People who get uncomfortable with the tension finally throw up their arms and say, "You know, things should just not be this way. They could be better!" And that's exactly what you want. ImpACT connects with that kind of people. They're the ones you want on your team because they're always pushing to get to the next level.

When God is striving to get our attention, He wants us unsettled. He wants us to embrace unresolved tension so we'll do great things for Him.

Hold On—Loosely

If you want to squelch people's desire to help you help others, then tighten your grip on them with a heavy hand, fingers touching everything they do. To squeeze the passion out of everyone involved, micromanage your ImpACT plans, don't trust your leaders, berate them over minor issues, and generally be in everyone's face as much as you can. You'll make their lives miserable and severely hamper your ImpACT campaign—for awhile. Then it will all be over.

Give people room to do their work, and trust them to do it. Correct when necessary, and praise people regularly. Above all, hold the reins loosely because at the end of the day, you are not in control—God is!

Youth Is Strength

There are no age limitations when it comes to who God uses to relieve suffering. At North Point, children and teens routinely join their parents in serving our community. Every summer, ImpACT is both promoted and carried out by our junior and senior high school students as they spend a week serving in local social justice organizations all over the community.

When you involve young people, you'll benefit from their natural energy, enthusiasm, and passion. And they will be blessed as they see themselves:

- Make a difference;

- Focus their attention on others;
- Put smiles on people's faces who can give nothing in return but a smile;
- Be a part of something bigger than themselves;
- Learn how to serve others;
- Minister to those who are hurting.

Perhaps best of all, you'll set them up for a lifetime of service to Christ.

> **"Everybody can be great. . . because anybody can serve. You don't have to have a college degree to serve. . . . You only need a heart full of grace. A soul generated by love."**[55]
>
> —Martin Luther King, Jr.

Holidays Are for Sharing

Nothing builds camaraderie among your volunteers like helping hurting people at special times of the year. At North Point, we always do something for our community at Christmas. We invite hundreds of impoverished families to the church to receive food, groceries, toys, portraits, medical and dental screenings, and time with Santa Claus. It's our way of saying, "Merry Christmas" to families who otherwise have little reason for joy during the holidays.

Combining Second Saturday outreaches with major holidays is an excellent way to connect with people. We've found that some holidays are better than others for reaching the people in our community, and you'll probably find this to be true as well. Just go with the flow, and don't feel compelled to do something at every holiday. Do what works. For instance, we generally give a financial gift to local social organizations in April (Easter), July (Independence Day), and November (Thanksgiving) because our volunteer families usually have less time to spare. School commitments, vacation time, and extended family gatherings tend to rule

---

55. Martin Luther King, http://mlk-kpp01.stanford.edu/index.php/encyclopedia/documentsentry/doc_the_drum_major_instinct/

at those times. And when we reach out to the community, we want to do it with excellence. So we wait until we're at full strength.

Remember Why You Embraced ImpACT

If you forget why you started ImpACT, you'll end up like a major league baseball player who holds out for millions of dollars rather than playing for the simple love of the game. Remember—and remind your workers—that you got into this because you love God and want to make a difference for Him in your community and the world.

Sometimes that will be the only thought that gets you and your people through the challenges you face. Sometimes that will be the only thing that keeps your people on mission. So find a way to regularly remind them why ImpACT is so important. Mention it every few weeks from the pulpit. Give a two-minute pep talk at Second Saturdays. And keep the vision alive on your church website, in newsletters, and through brief reports in the bulletin.

No End to the Opportunities

As your church makes inroads into your community, you will inspire other churches to the same. That's a good thing. Don't think of other churches as competitors. Recognize them as partners in the battle you've chosen to fight.

If you give away bikes and another church does too, that just means more kids have bikes. If you stock impoverished families with school supplies and shoes and another church does the same, praise God—fewer kids will be going to school this year without the supplies and confidence they need to do well in the classroom.

Your dream goal should be that every church gets on board with you so the churches become healthier and the community grows stronger. No matter how many churches join the fight, there will always be more people to help.

Jesus Wanted to Reach Everyone—Do You?

The church in America has a history of reaching mostly middle-class white people. But Jesus wants to reach everyone: the poor, suffering, diseased, hurt, addicted, and spiritually lost of every race and nationality.

God is depending on his Bride to do the groundwork that will draw people to a place where they want to begin a journey with Jesus. One of the best ways to do that is to reach into your community with tangible help and hope. Do that, and you'll make the ImpACT you and your church were created to make.

CHAPTER 10

THE IMPULSE FOR ACTION

Hopefully, by now you're feeling motivated to put into practice the ImpACT ideas I've shared. There's likely, though, one last significant question that remains. You wonder for yourself, your church, the people you lead: How will we fit this in?

I've mentioned the answer earlier in passing, but allow me to be very direct in this concluding chapter. The answer is: You won't.

ImpACT doesn't fit into your already existing world of church things to do. ImpACT requires a different mindset, and it has to be given its own priority in the mix of ministries and plans you're already involved in. "How to do it" can happen because of a God-created principle that applies to all of life and which is revolutionary when it comes to taking action on a vision as significant as ImpACT. I'll tell you how the principle answers the how-will-we-fit-this-in question, but first I need to explain a few things about a remarkable way God works.

Doing What You Believe

Some Bible verses—like John 3:16—are comforting. I prefer such scriptures that make me feel good. But some verses that are just as much part of the Bible can make your stomach churn with the challenges they present. Take James 4:17, for instance: "Anyone, then, who knows the good he ought to do and doesn't to it, sins."

"Sinning by not doing what we know is good" really raises the stakes for those of us who understand what God requires. He expects us to put our faith into action. When you put that directive alongside the global giants, it becomes obvious God's requirement is that we all do something.

The problem is, we Americans tend to have our lives full to overflowing with activities to occupy our time, drain our energy, and suck up our finances. There's no room to add anything. I fully acknowledge that this too-busyness is not just an excuse to avoid doing what we know we should. If I'm not careful, I can become just as overcommitted as the next guy—maybe even more so.

To this problem, though, I have found a remarkably simple solution, and I'm not one who tends to think in terms of simplistic answers. I believe life is full of complexities. Sometimes there are no blacks and whites, just a disturbing range of gray possibilities. But on this point of how to incorporate into your Christian walk the need to do the things that really matter, I can offer a simple solution, because God treats this area with such clarity. In fact, I've even got a formula for you, and here it is:

> *I simplify, then God will multiply, and that always results in margin.*

Margin. Margin is what gives you the time, energy, and resources to do what's important. It doesn't require that you add something to an already overflowing schedule. What it does require is that you make a decision to eliminate something that may be important in order to accommodate something that is even more important.

Once on a family trip to Colorado, I glimpsed how lack of margin creates stress. Trail Ridge Road twists its way from Estes Park, Colorado up through the crests of Rocky Mountain National Park, and I was the family chauffer for our ride there. My wife and children had a great day. They snapped pictures of awe-inspiring peaks, gawked at assorted big game, and cooed over how much snow still lay on the ground in summer. To them, it was all fun and relaxation. But I don't know when I've ever been more stressed out. Why? Because I was driving. On that road through the stratosphere, one wrong move behind the steering wheel, and everyone dies. Mountain roads along thousand-foot cliffs offer no margin for error. No margin = high stress. Too often, our lives are like that every day. Swerve off schedule even a little, and your plans are toast.

Lack of margin is not just a modern phenomenon. It's a lifestyle choice people have made throughout history. Jesus encountered margin-less people even among His friends. Martha was like that.

In Luke 10:38-42, Jesus visits two sisters for dinner. Martha can think of nothing but making sure all the preparations are "just so," and she scolds her sister, Mary—right in front of Jesus!—for ignoring the need to help. What is Mary doing instead? She's listening to Jesus, satisfying her hunger for spiritual food, recognizing that the only Source in the universe sits in her living room. What an opportunity! She's chosen the truly more important thing, and Jesus says so. He promises, in fact, that her choosing what matters will never be taken away from her. She'll always have the treasure of Jesus' words and the experience of His presence in her heart and mind. Mary had margin. She made room for the most important things. Martha had none. She settled for what was urgent, not essential.

The amazing thing is that when we put first things first, in God's economy—of time, money, energy, creativity, possibilities—we end up with more of what we need. Hopefully, you've discovered, for example, that faithfulness to tithing makes it possible to live better on the remaining 90 percent than you would have on the un-tithed 100 percent. That's an application of the simplification principle in finances. It applies to other ways of pursuing God, too.

I've talked with people who complain that they'd like to grow spiritually, but they don't have time to include Bible reading and prayer time in their daily routine. And it's true. Many of them don't have time to add that to an overwhelmed schedule. If you're already getting up at 5 A.M. to get everything done, there's not much chance you have the energy to start waking at 4:30 for Bible study and prayer. No, that's not going to work.

What will work is to delete something else less important (because everything else is less important than your relationship with God) in order to have time with the Lord. You see, whatever you give God first of, He multiplies. In every area of life, you must cut out the merely important things to make room for the most important things.

Simplifying at Church

Let me wrap up with an example of how we put this principle to work on a church-wide scale at North Point. Part of what led us to ImpACT was the realization that reaching people is the most essential action we could possibly pursue. As we evaluated how to do that, we identified the need to add a worship service on Saturday. The problem is that we already had a weekly agenda packed with activities. And since everything we do is ministry-oriented, it was easy to argue that everything was important, and we didn't have time to add anything to the schedule.

At first, we were tempted to simply add a service. I'm sure if we had tried, though, it would have done nothing but burn out our highly motivated staff and discourage the people in our church who most want to do what is right. We realized that something else had to go. In a difficult—and to some people, controversial—decision, we eliminated our Wednesday Night New Community Service.

As important as that event had been to us, it was not as important as reaching new people in the way we felt God challenging us to do. But we did it. We gave ourselves the margin to cut one thing out of our schedule and add something more crucial. And the principle kicked in. When we simplified, God multiplied, and we began to reach more people than ever. Sure, some folks were not happy with church leadership, but it was what we had to do to be doing the right thing. And we've never been sorry. God has multiplied—as I've shared over and over in this book—our church in many ways.

God's Plan for Your Life

Putting faith into action is at the core of God's plan for the life of every believer and church body. In a nutshell, His goal is this: God is doing His best to turn you and your church into fully devoted followers of Christ. Fully devoted followers do, as best they know how, whatever Jesus would do.

He wants you to make a difference.

Do you have the heart to reach people who have never been reached? How badly do you want to stop talking about reaching people and really do it? Will you delete from the life of your church the important things you're doing in order to make room for what is crucial?

If you want it badly enough, now is the time for a revolution. As you embark on ImpACT, let God make you obsessed with introducing people to Jesus outside the walls of church.

It's too easy to trundle along and do nothing. To change the world, you must be intentional about changing the way you do what you do. You'll likely have to scratch from your church or personal agenda something you think is important (if you didn't think it was important, why would you be doing it in the first place?) in order to take on something even more important. But if you do, I guarantee the change will delight your spirit, edify your church, and revolutionize your community.

You will have an ImpACT.

We've done it at North Point and have no regrets. In fact, we can't imagine doing church any other way. Our lives have soared (with wings like eagles!) as we've seen others' lives transformed. I would be doing you a disservice if I didn't encourage you to do as Jesus said of the Good Samaritan: "Go and do likewise."

GLOSSARY OF TERMS

Biblical Social Justice—A concept which propels Christ followers to love and help the poor and suffering like Jesus did.

Christ Follower—Someone who has made life change by committing his or her life to Christ.

Compassion—A feeling of deep sympathy and sorrow for another who is stricken by misfortune, accompanied by a strong desire to alleviate the suffering.[56]

DNA—The stuff inside ImpACT that makes it work.

Global Giants—Scourges in your community and around the world that rob people of finances, health, life, and freedom.

ImpACT—A strategic outreach to fight the four global giants of disease, poverty, illiteracy, and spiritual emptiness that affect local and global communities.

Modern-day Pharisees (MDPs)—People associated with churches who are more concerned about dogma and rules than helping people and letting the Holy Spirit do His work.

Second Saturday—Community outreach event where volunteers from a church spend four hours helping a social justice organization do a major project that will make the organization more effective in its work.

Social Justice Partners—Local or international organizations that are fighting the global giants your church is targeting.

---

56. Dictionary.com

SOME OF NORTH POINT CHURCH'S SOCIAL JUSTICE PARTNERS

Down Syndrome Group of the Ozarks

Down Syndrome Group of the Ozarks is an organization made up of parents, professionals and other interested parties committed to creating an extensive network of support for individuals with Down syndrome and those who love and serve them in Southwest Missouri. They help individuals with Down syndrome become successful by providing support and education to loving families, bringing awareness of early intervention services, promoting inclusive education, highlighting appropriate medical services, encouraging quality employment opportunities, and advocating for community awareness and acceptance (see www.ozarksdsg.org).

Convoy of Hope

Since its founding as a 501(c)3 non-profit organization in 1994, Convoy of Hope has served more than 42 million people throughout the world via its international children's feeding initiatives, community outreaches, disaster response, and partner resourcing. There are more than 89,000 children in Convoy's feeding initiative in El Salvador, Haiti, Honduras, Kenya, Nicaragua, and the Philippines. The food program provides good nutrition, clean and safe drinking water, instruction on agricultural techniques, teaching about healthy living environments, as well as general education. Convoy of Hope is consistently lauded for the effectiveness and efficiency of its work to mobilize tens of thousands of volunteers for community outreaches and for assistance during times of disaster response (see www.convoyofhope.org).

AIDS Project of the Ozarks

AIDS Project of the Ozarks is a non-profit, community-based organization serving a 29-county region in southwest Missouri. APO assists over 600 HIV/AIDS sufferers and their families. Concerned families and friends established the organization as a grass roots entity in 1983. Services include: medical care, case management, education for the general public, and services to persons with HIV infection, their families, and significant others in a confidential, caring environment (see www.aidsprojectoftheozarks.org).

Chi Alpha

Chi Alpha reaches college students on campuses nationwide. Through its ministry facilities and staff, the organization provides discipleship programs, evangelistic outreaches, and on-campus worship opportunities.

Boys & Girls Club

The primary mission of the Boys & Girls Clubs of Springfield is to enhance the quality of life for its youthful participants. With special concern for the disadvantaged, the Boys & Girls Clubs help youth to help themselves and realize their potential for growth and development. Aware of influences in the total environment, the Boys & Girls Clubs provide youth with relevant and diversified individual and group services. Its activities demonstrate that adults care for youth and truly desire to help them grow into productive people with the skills necessary for living well. Its programs include principles of behavioral guidance which will achieve the health, social, educational, vocational, character, and leadership development of its members (see www.bgclubspringfield.org).

IMPACT SAMPLE PROMOTION MATERIALS

This flyer is used all year round to promote ImpACT.

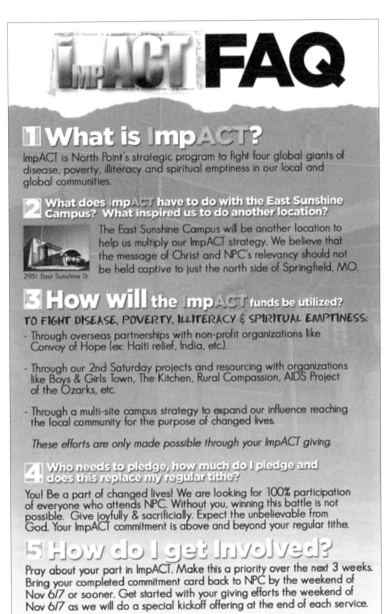

ImpACT FAQ

1 What is ImpACT?

ImpACT is North Point's strategic program to fight four global giants of disease, poverty, illiteracy and spiritual emptiness in our local and global communities.

2 What does ImpACT have to do with the East Sunshine Campus? What inspired us to do another location?

The East Sunshine Campus will be another location to help us multiply our ImpACT strategy. We believe that the message of Christ and NPC's relevancy should not be held captive to just the north side of Springfield, MO.

2951 East Sunshine St.

3 How will the ImpACT funds be utilized?

TO FIGHT DISEASE, POVERTY, ILLITERACY & SPIRITUAL EMPTINESS:

- Through overseas partnerships with non-profit organizations like Convoy of Hope (ex: Haiti relief, India, etc.).

- Through our 2nd Saturday projects and resourcing with organizations like Boys & Girls Town, The Kitchen, Rural Compassion, AIDS Project of the Ozarks, etc.

- Through a multi-site campus strategy to expand our influence reaching the local community for the purpose of changed lives.

These efforts are only made possible through your ImpACT giving.

4 Who needs to pledge, how much do I pledge and does this replace my regular tithe?

You! Be a part of changed lives! We are looking for 100% participation of everyone who attends NPC. Without you, winning this battle is not possible. Give joyfully & sacrificially. Expect the unbelievable from God. Your ImpACT commitment is above and beyond your regular tithe.

5 How do I get Involved?

Pray about your part in ImpACT. Make this a priority over the next 3 weeks. Bring your completed commitment card back to NPC by the weekend of Nov 6/7 or sooner. Get started with your giving efforts the weekend of Nov 6/7 as we will do a special kickoff offering at the end of each service.

These are example pledge cards we have used over the last couple of years since starting the campaign. Every year, we change it up a little bit, but use the same basic "look" so it builds a consistent image for ImpACT.

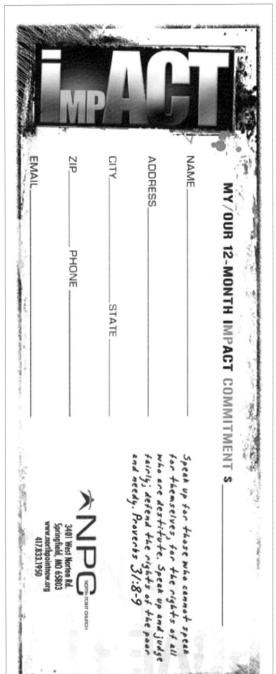

These flyers are handed out in the bulletin for the 3-week ImpACT series. We have changed these every year as well but have maintained a consistent concept.

Series 1

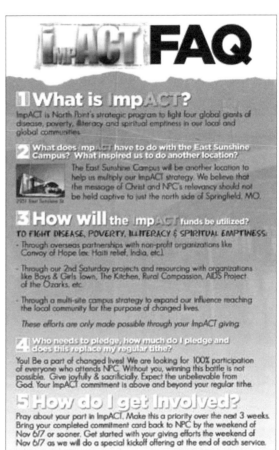

2LOCATIONSONE

iMPACT

FIGHTING
POVERTY
SPIRITUAL
EMPTINESS
ILLITERACY
DISEASE

A FEW HIGHLIGHTS OF 2010'S IMPACT PROGRAM –
2ND SATURDAY AND FINANCIAL CONTRIBUTIONS

Partnered with Convoy of Hope, Champion Athletes of the Ozarks, Family Violence Center, Rural Compassion, AIDS Project of the Ozarks, Boys & Girls Town, Boys & Girls Club, OACAC, The Kitchen and Local Public Schools

HOW WE MADE AN IMPACT...

+ Gave out **1000+** shoes, socks and underwear
+ ~~Handed to kids towels shirts, back~~
+ Provided a church home for many families after they attended an outreach event
+ Benefited **hundreds** of NPC families in need
+ ~~Provided a makeover at Family Violence Center & The Kitchen in their game rooms for a place to relax and take their mind off of hardships in their lives~~
+ ~~Built self esteem and self confidence in women & kids who were homeless, sick & disadvantaged~~
+ Packed & supplied over **100** backpacks with school supplies
+ Provided **450** turkey dinners to families in need
+ Changed out & supplied new bedding & bath items to teens at The Kitchen
+ Served **5000** drinks, **3750** cookies, **2000** chips, **3720** hot dogs
+ Provided a makeover to a local school, painting classrooms, washing windows, tree trimming, painting playground equipment and more
+ Provided approx. **300** haircuts and over **150** medical check-ups
+ ~~Packed over 75,000 meals which will feed 212 children for 1 year~~
+ Funded Convoy of Hope for Haiti Relief
+ ~~Provided new bedding for kids at Boys & Girls Town~~

2LOCATIONSONE iMPACT **2nd Campus: East Sunshine**
2 CAMPUSES MAKING A LARGE IMPACT IN THE COMMUNITY!

+ Over **12,000** square feet of building space
+ **200 GALLONS OF PAINT TO PAINT AND RENOVATE NEW BUILDING**
+ **PROVIDING THE EAST SIDE OF TOWN WITH A RELEVANT MESSAGE OF CHRIST**
+ Under construction w/ **3800** man hours to get building ready for launch!
+ **PREPPING FOR AWESOME KID & STUDENT PROGRAMS**
+ Getting ready for live music & video teaching with digital audio, radical lighting & big screens!
+ **GET READY FOR A COUNTLESS NUMBER OF CHANGED LIVES!**

Series 2

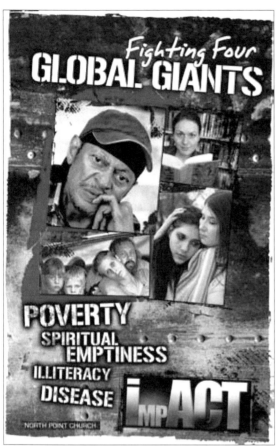

Series 3

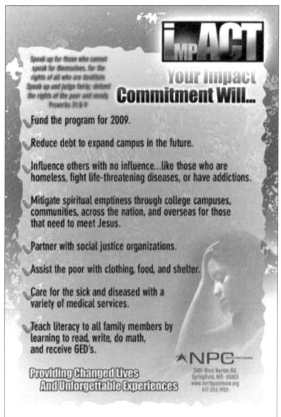

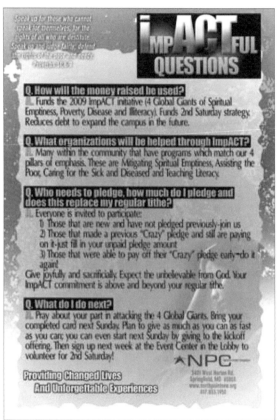

After people have made their pledge on the last weekend, we send a follow-up thank you letter like this one.

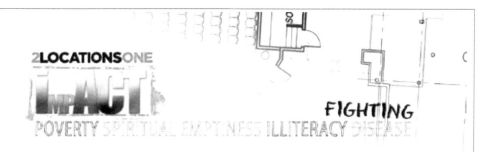

2LOCATIONSONE

FIGHTING

POVERTY SPIRITUAL EMPTINESS ILLITERACY DISEASE

Wednesday, November 10, 2010

Dear John and Jane,

The Changed Life Celebration that concluded our 3-week ▓▓▓ series was one of the most powerful experiences I've had since we started North Point Church in 2003. It's not every day that I'm moved to tears, but I was this weekend. Although there was only a handful of NPC'ers that we could fit on the stage for each service, there is no doubt that all of us have a Changed Life story to celebrate!

As of today, $611,000 has been pledged for ▓▓▓ – Praise God! I am proud of North Point and thankful to you and others who have stepped up to this faith challenge. Our needed miracle amount is over $700,000 and the more we raise, the more we can do.

Your pledge for **$1500** will be an example to others as your compassion will be seen through the difference, together, we can make towards life change. I have included your commitment card as a prayer reminder and expectation of what God is ready to do through your faithfulness.

I trust that this is as much of a challenge to you as it is to me. For me personally, I find it helpful to pay as much towards my pledge as fast as I can and let God provide. Providing *life change* at the very core of need, that is what I really believe individuals and churches exist to do.

You can make a difference. But **we** can do something revolutionary and strategic. Through ▓▓▓ we do together what we couldn't do as individuals.

God has something supernatural He wants to do in your life.

Grateful to be your pastor,

Tommy

NORTH POINT CHURCH
3401 W. NORTON ROAD, SPRINGFIELD, MISSOURI 65803
PHONE 417.833.1950 FAX 417.833.0040 WWW.NORTHPOINTNOW.ORG

Throughout the year, we send quarterly updates to those who have pledged. The letter shows the current amount that they have given towards ImpACT. Here is an example letter.

2LOCATIONSONE

FIGHTING

POVERTY SPIRITUAL EMPTINESS ILLITERACY DISEASE

Attendee Name   04/11/11
Address
City, State Zip

Dear Smith Family,

Your ImpACT pledge in November allowed us to make commitments to outreach projects throughout the community for 2011. The follow-through in our outreach projects and financial support months are now contingent on your contributions the rest of this year.

We are excited about the difference you make with your commitment and also how God will work through your life to help you pay your pledge. Below is your update on your total pledge, how much you have contributed, and how much you have to go to pay off your pledge by November 2011. Together we are making an impact on our community and communities around the world. If you have any questions, please email us at info@northpointchurch.tv or call us at 417-833-1950.

Your ImpACT Pledge And ImpACT Giving Records From November 2010 Through 4/11/11):

Total Pledged	Total Given	Amount To-Go (by Nov 2011)
$1000	$450	$550

Since November 2010, through your ImpACT giving we have:
- ❖ Provided a 1000+ disadvantaged people groceries, turkeys, flu shots, haircuts, toys and an unforgettable experience for Christmas!
- ❖ Provided financial support to Convoy of Hope so they could further their work in areas devastated by natural disasters!
- ❖ Opened our East Sunshine campus, allowing us to make an even bigger ImpACT in our community!
- ❖ Made 78,484 meals for starving children!
- ❖ Provided education, fun and financial support to three organizations in the Ozarks that serve thousands of individuals affected by disabilities!
- ❖ Made history with donating enough blood to save as much as 900+ lives!

Let's continue to make an ImpACT together,

Pastor Tommy

NORTH POINT CHURCH
3401 W. NORTON ROAD, SPRINGFIELD, MISSOURI 65803
PHONE 417.833.1950   FAX 417.833.0040   WWW.NORTHPOINTCHURCH.TV

Each month for ImpACT, we send out either a postcard or letter reminding people to give to ImpACT. Here are a couple of examples.

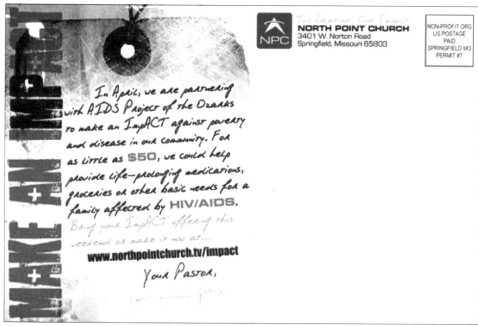

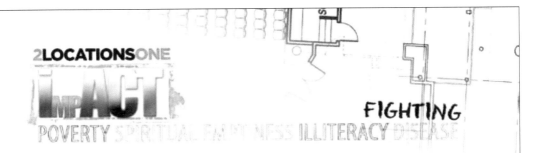

2LOCATIONSONE

ImpACT

FIGHTING

POVERTY SPIRITUAL EMPTINESS ILLITERACY DISEASE

February 28, 2011

Dear Smith Family,

Did you know that 1 in every 800-1,000 live births is a child with Down syndrome? Did you know that people with Down syndrome (DS) go to college? Live independently? Are employed as artists, actors, child care workers? Most of us do not think of these things on a regular basis. We tend to believe that Down syndrome is a rare genetic disorder or that those with DS will have severe developmental or intellectual delays. And it's just not true! Many people diagnosed with DS or other developmental or intellectual disabilities have great potential when given the opportunity to succeed.

In March, North Point Church has the opportunity to partner with Down Syndrome Group of the Ozarks, Champion Athletes of the Ozarks and Special Olympics of Missouri to make a difference in the lives of those with Down syndrome or other developmental or intellectual disabilities. These organizations make it their mission to provide their target audience with self-esteem, encouragement, friendships & much more. We want to raise them up in these efforts by making you and the rest of the community aware of them!

On March 12, 2011, North Point Church is hosting Xtreme Games & Expos for those associated with the groups above. This event is part of our ImpACT program and 2nd Saturday events hosted on the 2nd Saturday of almost each month. ImpACT is NPC's outreach strategy to fight the four global giants of disease, poverty, illiteracy and spiritual emptiness. To attack these giants, we partner with local non-profit organizations like those above in and around Springfield, MO. ImpACT is part of the DNA of North Point Chruch. We live and breathe it.

We know we are called to, "Speak up for those who can't speak for themselves, for the rights of all who are destitute. Speak up and judge fairly; defend the rights of the poor and needy." – Proverbs 31:8-9

 NORTH POINT CHURCH
■ 3401 W. NORTON ROAD, SPRINGFIELD, MISSOURI 65803
NPC ■ PHONE 417.833.1950 ■ FAX 417.833.0040 ■ WWW.NORTHPOINTCHURCH.TV

2LOCATIONSONE

FIGHTING

POVERTY SPIRITUAL EMPTINESS ILLITERACY DISEASE

ImpACT and 2nd Saturday events happen because North Point Church partners together financially. **Every dollar we give to ImpACT makes our ImpACT in the community bigger.** Make a difference with the resources God has given us and speak up for those who can't speak for themselves.

I want to thank you in advance for being a part of this effort. ImpACT is changing lives and it is beautiful. What an awesome thing to be a part of! I can't wait to see what happens in March at this event – it will be life changing for all.

Making an ImpACT together,

Adam
Resource Director

3 Easy Ways To Give To ImpACT This Week!!!
- ❖ Give now at www.northpointchurch.tv/giving
- ❖ Use your bank's online bill pay system to have a check sent to NPC
- ❖ Use the enclosed tithe envelope for this weekend's offering

NORTH POINT CHURCH
■ 3401 W. NORTON ROAD, SPRINGFIELD, MISSOURI 65803
■ PHONE 417.833.1950 ■ FAX 417.833.0040 ■ WWW.NORTHPOINTCHURCH.TV

In July, ImpACT is partnering with Good Samaritan Boys Ranch! We are making a $40,000+ investment in this project... A gift of $50 or more will help provide the much needed renovations to their campus and care packages to boys who are striving to make a life change. You can change the life of a child! Bring your ImpACT offering this weekend or make it now at www.northpointchurch.tv/impact

Your Pastor,

After a contributor pays off his or her pledge, we send a thank you letter such as this one.

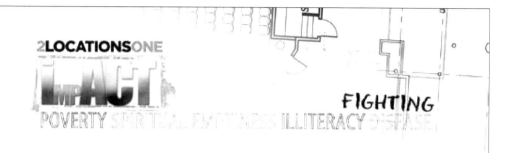

Wednesday, April 20, 2011

John Smith
1515 North Point Ave
Springfield, MO 65803

Dear John,

On behalf of North Point Church, I would like to thank you for paying off your pledge to ImpACT. ImpACT has been able to change more lives than ever imagined, and this would not have been possible without sacrificial generosity.

Each year, North Point continues to advance its mission of making a larger impact in the community. Through ImpACT, along with your giving, we have been able to expand our influence in our neighborhood, and around the world. From partnering with Convoy of Hope to Boys & Girls Town to Special Olympics of Missouri (and many more!), we are making a difference all around the globe – starting right here in Springfield, MO.

There is so much more we can do in this community as we live out our faith (feed those that are starving, provide shoes for the disadvantaged, care for those that are sick, etc.). Your dollars are multiplied through ImpACT.

Thank you again for the generous support of ImpACT!

Making an ImpACT together,

Tommy Sparger
Lead Pastor

NORTH POINT CHURCH
■ 3401 W. NORTON ROAD, SPRINGFIELD, MISSOURI 65803
■ PHONE 417.833.1950 ■ FAX 417.833.0040 ■ WWW.NORTHPOINTCHURCH.TV

IMPACT 2ND SATURDAY SAMPLE MATERIALS

Calendar of Events

Influence those who have no influence
Mitigate **spiritual emptiness**
Partner with social justice orgs
Assist the **Poor**
Care of the **sick and diseased**
Teach **Literacy**

2nd Saturday
CALENDAR of EVENTS 2010

DATE & TIME	SOCIAL JUSTICE ORG	LOCATION	CONTACT	GLOBAL GIANT(S)/PROJECT IDEA
Jan. 9, 2010	Convoy of Hope	Convoy of Hope	Jim	Assist the poor, sick/diseased, spiritual emptiness. "Feed My Starving Children" Project.
Feb. 13, 2010	Champion Athletes of the Ozarks	B&G Club	Angelah	Care for the sick/diseased, spiritual emptiness. Olympics Project.
Mar. 13, 2010	Family Violence Center	FVC/North Point Church	Rich	Assist the poor, spiritual emptiness. Relationship Building Day/Work Project.
Apr. 10, 2010	Aids Project of the Ozarks	<u>Non-Event Resource</u>	Michael	Assist the poor, sick/diseased, spiritual emptiness.
May 8, 2010	B&G Town	B&G Town	Millie	Assist the poor and spiritual emptiness. Relationship Building Day/Work Project.
Jun. 12, 2010	School Makeover	Local Elementary School	Leslie	Assist the poor, spiritual emptiness, maybe literacy Work Project.
Jul. 10, 2010	Ozarks Literacy Council	<u>Non-Event Resource</u>	Tim	Assist the poor, literacy
Aug. 14, 2010	Back 2 School	NPC		Assist the poor, sick/diseased, spiritual emptiness. Giveaway/Fun Day.
Sep. 11, 2010	B&G Clubs	<u>Non-Event Resource</u>	Andrew	Assist the poor, sick/diseased, spiritual emptiness.
Oct. 9, 2010	The Kitchen	The Kitchen	Patty	Assist the poor, sick/diseased, spiritual emptiness. Relationship Building Day/Work Project.
Nov. 13, 2010	Rural Compassion	North Point Church	Jim	Assist the poor, sick/diseased, spiritual emptiness, literacy. MATCH "CAMPAIGN" TIME. Work Project (Disaster Buckets, Clothing Supply, Book Binding, Etc).
Dec. 11, 2010	Christmas Giveaway	NPC		Assist the poor, spiritual emptiness. Giveaway/Fun Day.

Partnership Invitation Letter

Dear Potential Partner,

You are receiving this letter due to your recent inquiry in partnering with North Point Church (NPC) in the sharing of resources – either financially, through volunteers or promotion.

I am a Director at North Point Church and one of my responsibilities is identifying potential outreach partners in the Ozarks that will help us with our ImpACT initiative. ImpACT is North Point Church's strategic outreach in which we target the 4 GLOBAL GIANTS of disease, poverty, illiteracy, and spiritual emptiness that are affecting our local communities as well as the global community.

Our ImpACT outreach events take place on a monthly basis. Outreach events (that we call "2nd Saturday") are facilitated within 30 minutes of NPC's campus so that we can bus volunteers from campus, provide them enough time to properly complete their projects and then bus them back. Our 2nd Saturday events engage 300-400 volunteers at a time for up to 3 hours.

The vision of ImpACT was put on the hearts of NPC's leadership team in 2008. Since implementing this strategy it has been transformational for our volunteers and community. Through our ImpACT strategy we are showing our volunteers how a church can be a beacon of light in its local community so that one day those same volunteers understand how we can be a beacon of light in the USA and across the globe. In order for us to properly resource ImpACT we discontinued the funding of projects outside of the church campus that did not meet ImpACT's requirements.

The ImpACT initiative is North Point Church's mission's strategy. We wholeheartedly believe in what individual missionaries are doing at home and around the globe, and we pray for their safety and their work for God's kingdom. We also believe real humanitarian needs exist in our own backyard and that a very unique and special opportunity exists for NPC to plug its volunteers into regular situations in which they can live out their faith and speak for those who are struggling in our very own community.

To discuss a potential partnership with NPC's ImpACT initiative organizations must:
1) Have projects that will engage 300-400 volunteers for 3 hours on the morning of a Saturday (specifically the 2nd Saturday of the month), and
2) Help us target at least one of our four global giants (disease, poverty, illiteracy & spiritual emptiness).

We typically finalize our partnerships in January of each year. If you are contacting us after January we will likely need to look at a potential partnership in the following calendar year. If you feel your organization could partner with ImpACT based on these requirements, please contact me personally to discuss it further.

If you have any other questions about a partnership, please feel free to contact me.

Grateful for your interest,

Your Name
2nd Saturday Director
North Point Church – (417) 833-1950
youremail@northpointnow.org

Event Worksheet

2ND SATURDAY EVENT WORKSHEET

Event:
Partner Organization:
Date/Time/Place:
Guests & Scope & Goals:
Global Giants Tackled:

3 Months Out		
✓	Fac.	Task
		Start an **Event Worksheet**
		Meet with partner to determine scope
		Create and confirm Project Budget
		Charter Buses
		Prepare **Video Request Form** for Media

2 Months Out		
✓	Fac.	Task
		Collect mailing list from partner
		Design invitations
		Print and mail invitations
		Prepare **Event Request Form** for Facilities Team
		Visit partner for B-roll
		Order supplies & purchases needed

1 Month Out		
✓	Fac.	Task
		Print and mail invitations – if needed 2nd round
		Secure any 3rd party rentals
		Load event info onto website
		New sign-up sheets in lobby
		Continuous count of vols & guests
		Select and secure leaders and providers
		Prepare Press Release
		Distribute (& collect) Changed Life bags
		Create detailed action plan
		Create event signage
		3 wks out - video promotion at church
		3 wks out – decide on and invite leaders

Week Of		
✓	Fac.	Task
		Review Meeting
		Send out **Press Release** 3x; radio?
		Confirm leaders and providers
		Postcard reminder to volunteers
		Compare # volunteers to # guests; adjust plan
		Print registration sheets
		Create and email **Site Leader Notes** & **Floor Plan**
		Create **Bus Leader Packets**
		Final purchases needed
		Decorating, Signage, Pre-assembly, Name tags, etc
		Deliveries, if off-site
TBD		Thursday night meeting with leaders

Day Of		
✓	Fac.	Task
		Meet with leaders and preview areas
		Bus leaders prep buses
		Rally with volunteers
		Travel, setup, execute, video, clean up
		Recap meeting (immediately after event)

Week After		
✓	Fac.	Task
		Complete **Stat Sheet**
		Thank you notes to leaders and providers
		Show recap video at church
		Load recap video & pictures onto website

Bold indicates a document

Reminder Email to Volunteers (sent 3 days before event)

Subject: Reminder – This Saturday, Joplin Help!

Hi {FirstName}!

We are excited for you to be a part of this coming weekend to make an ImpACT in Joplin!

If you are receiving this email, you have signed up to attend the event to help Joplin this coming Saturday, June 4 @ 8am.

Important Reminders & Information:

- *Arrive at North Point Church, Norton Road, at 8am SHARP!*
- **Volunteers MUST BE 10 or older to participate.**
- *You MUST BE REGISTERED for this event to attend as there is limited space.*
- **Wear comfortable, closed toe shoes and work clothes as we will be in a warehouse setting.**
- *You MUST ride the bus on the way to and from the event.*

Thank you for being a part of Changed Lives!

See you there,

The ImpACT Team

End of Event Evaluation Form

Evaluation Form

1) How did the event turn out?

2) Which leaders were most effective? Which leaders were not effective?

3) How was the partner to work with? Should we work with again? Why or why not?

4) Were the volunteers fulfilled? If yes, why? If not, why not?

5) Did we have enough supplies?

6) What can we do different next time to make better?

Example 1: Back to School Event (partnered with local schools, Boys & Girls Club, other organizations)

We send out a press release similar to this one approximately 1 week in advance of the event as well as on the day of the event.

FOR IMMEDIATE RELEASE: August 2, 2010
CONTACT: Adam, Resource Director
(###) ###-#### | adam@northpointnow.org

Back to School Bash to Help 1,000 Ozark Children In Need

SPRINGFIELD, MO - On Saturday, August 14 as many as 1,000 elementary students (of families experiencing financial difficulties) will visit 3401 W Norton Rd as North Point Church (NPC) volunteers put on a Back 2 School Bash. From 9am to 11am, nearly 300 volunteer workers will be giving out shoes, socks, underwear and groceries. There will also be medical professionals and hairstylists volunteering their time to provide free dental checks, physicals and haircuts to students Kindergarten through 5th grade. Registration is currently 100% full due to current demand. The outdoor carnival is open to anyone who would like to attend, even if a family is not registered.

The Back 2 School Bash is a part of NPC's ImpACT program; designed to attack the four global giants of disease, illiteracy, poverty and spiritual emptiness. On the 2nd Saturday of each month, NPC partners with a local community organization to meet their needs with no strings attached. For this event, NPC worked with local schools and other non-profits to help identify children that may be in need of these items.

In addition to the giveaways, children and their families will be able to enjoy fun activities like a theater show, fire truck, Black Hawk helicopter, barbeque and a carnival area with lots of games.

"Right now is an opportunity for the local church to serve families that are struggling to make it," says Adam, Resource Director at NPC. "Being a kid is difficult enough and it's not a child's fault if they can't replace their worn-out shoes, socks, underwear or get a haircut. We think providing a fun environment and needed resources to these children is a help to our community that inspires more of us to step up and help. We are encouraging everyone at NPC to do what they can to make an impact. When we help someone and don't expect anything in return it lets people know in a real, tangible way that we care about them."

North Point Church is led by Pastor Tommy and reaches over 4,000 in weekly attendance. If you, or your organization, would like to get involved with NPC's monthly Impact program please contact Adam at ###-###-#### or info@northpointnow.org; or visit *www.northpointnow.org/impact*.

###

An Event Timeline helps it stay on track, making sure you start at 8am and end at 12pm (other than that, you can be somewhat flexible).

August Back 2 School Event
Timeline 08.14.10

Volunteers arrive	8:00 A.M.
Open store	9:00 - 10:00 A.M.
Family Theater	9:30-10:00 A.M.
Family Theater	10:00-10:30 A.M.
Carnival, haircuts, medical services, groceries	9:30-11:30 A.M.
Volunteer cleanup	11:30-Noon
Prepare building for Saturday service	Noon-5:00 P.M.

Rally Notes (use these to rally participants and pray together when all volunteers arrive at the church before the event).

Rally Notes

- Celebrate New Volunteers
- Back 2 School Bash – no strings attached: Store, Haircuts, Medical, Carnival, Food, Family Theater
- Don't eat the food until event is over.
- Pray
- Dismissal

Dismissal Order

Area	Leader(s)	Number = 450	Number = 350	Number = 250
Store	Mike & Susie Travis & Jessa	75	75	50
Groceries	Sharon	25	15	10
Security/Trash/ Parking	Jim Jason	15	10	10
Food Area	Angie	10	5	5
Medical	Melanie	0	0	0
Hair	Ken & Mindy	10	8	5
Family Theater	Tony Colette	5	5	5
Carnival (singlelife area)	Damon Amanda	35	30	25
Lobby Hosts	Tyler & Jada Dan & Patty	255	155	130
Greeters	Richard & Margaret Richard & Katie	8	5	0
Registration	Scott & Angie Justin & Jami	9	9	9

Some volunteers will be handpicked ahead of time… they are in red.

Aaron, Shawn, Chester, Richie, Jim, Jason= Parking Lot

Leader Notes (email these to leaders 1 week before event).

Leader Notes
Back To School Bash August 14, 2010

PARTNER   Springfield & Willard Public Schools, Boys & Girls Club, NPC Attendees, OACAC.

GOAL   The BIG picture is "CHANGED LIVES!" We are fighting the global giants of poverty and spiritual emptiness that are affecting our local community by providing an enjoyable morning for the children, while also meeting their practical needs for clothing and hygiene/medical care.

SCOPE   "Store" offering with shoes, underwear and toys, Family Theatre experience, medical & dental services, haircutting services, food, carnival, attractions, and take-home groceries.

SCHEDULE

7:30am –	Parking Lot staff in place
7:30am –	Leaders meet with their Supervisors
8:00am –	Volunteers arrive
8:05am –	Rally led by Adam
8:15am –	Dismissal / Leaders help count and lead volunteers to areas
8:30am –	Volunteers in place for set up
9:00am –	Registration Opens
9:00-11:30am –	**Event Open! (Store, Carnival, Everything Open At This Time)**
11:30am –	Clean up

INSTRUCTIONS PER AREA:
Danny – Adam's sidekick for the day!

Parking Lot/Outdoor Security/ Trash (10-15)
Leaders: Jim; Jason
Reports to: Rick M: ###-####
Please communicate to your team: why we are doing what we are doing, we're here for the common good, and stay busy.

- Direct traffic and parking, patrol area, security, pick up trash.

Greeters (0-8)
Leaders: Margaret & Richard; Richard & Katie
Reports to: Jamie M: ###-####
Please communicate to your team: why we are doing what we are doing, we're here for the common good, and stay busy.

- When families start arriving, send up to 8 volunteers outside/throughout lines to chat and mingle.
- There will be a non-registered booth for non-registered to check-in at to receive a FAQ sheet, Zone Pass, and Grocery Pass (will be explained later).
- To keep the air conditioning in, please facilitate entrance to the building in groups of 10-20. Only 1 set of doors will be open to help with the air – the guests will appreciate it when they are inside!
- Those with their registration cards should move to front of lines.
- You guys will have a bullhorn to stand on box making announcements and directing people.

Registration (9)
Leaders: Angie & Scott; Justin & Jami; Lane & Angie, Lobby
Reports to: Jamie M: ###-####
Please communicate to your team: why we are doing what we are doing, we're here for the common good, and stay busy.

- Prepare check-in counters.
- Hand out "money" for each item to kids as they check-in and one grocery pass per kid that is registered.
- If they have card, take card and let them go in. No card, look for their name on the registration sheets. Check them off. If they are not on list, they need to go outside to non-registered booth.
- Pair them up with host (host leaders will be helping with this too).
- Send them into store.
- Help get lobby back together.

Hosts (130-250)
Leaders: Tyler & Jada; Dan & Patty
Reports to: Jamie M: ###-####
Please communicate to your team: why we are doing what we are doing, we're here for the common good, and stay busy.

- Take 2-4 groups of volunteers through the building. Talk to them about things to talk about, how to handle guests.
- Hosts to smile and escort guests quickly thru the first half of the activities (store, Family Theatre, Medical/Dental, and Haircutting) then release them to go out to the carnival. Do not wait for guests while they are in medical or hair.
- Return to host another family. Engage in friendly conversation and give guests a heads up as to what services are coming up next, with everything being optional.
- Head out to carnival to visit with guests you hosted earlier.

Store (50-75)
Leaders: Brian & Maggie; Travis & Jessa, Main Auditorium
Reports to: Jamie M: ###-####
Please communicate to your team: why we are doing what we are doing, we're here for the common good, and stay busy.

- Tables will already be in place. Set up store: pull out changed life bags, divide between girls & boys, have people put out on table in organized fashion. 3 tables for each gender – share socks & underwear in same row.
- Children will have "money" to pick out items. In the event a size is not available in shoes, leader should go over and double check. If no size, then they can give out gift card. Do not advertise gift cards, as they are limited. Be as discreet as possible.
- Clean up @ 11am. Put tables in kitchen storage area.
- Pick out 15 volunteers to stay and help vacuum and put chairs back out. Stuff & straighten seatbacks. Kevin Holm should be the one to help lead with this clean-up.

Family Theatre (5)
Leaders: Dan; Tony; Colette & Darrin, Youth Auditorium
Reports to: Jamie M: ###-####
Please communicate to your team: why we are doing what we are doing , we're here for the common good, and stay busy.

- This year it's *come-and-go* style, no sitting through presentations but we will put up chairs.
- Keep flow moving through area.
- Have fun!
- Clean up chairs, set up for weekend services. Joey should be the one to help lead this clean-up.

Medical (0-have enough medical staff)
Leaders: Melanie, Kid Point Elementary Area
Reports to: Lisa M: ###-####
Please communicate to your team: why we are doing what we are doing, we're here for the common good, and stay busy.

- Get tables & chairs and set up in medical rooms, in front of each "office," and in the waiting room.
- Fold Sports Physical Sheets and cut Dental Check Sheets, put together bags with toothbrushes and toothpaste and Area Clinics handout.
- Pair up NPs & PAs with RNs & LPNs to work as teams.
- Facilitate an organized and timely movement of people, first-come, first-serve.
- Feel free to service adults, with children being the priority. We cannot treat "sick" individuals without a doctor present.
- Turn in lists for our records (numbers only, just to see how helping/what need is/etc).
- Clean up and put everything back in its place. Rick will be in place to help lead clean-up of this area.

- If you have additional North Point volunteers participate that are in the medical field, please collect their contact info for future reference.

Haircutting (6-8)
Leaders: Ken & Mindy, Kid Point Preschool Area
Reports to: Lisa M: ###-####
Please communicate to your team: why we are doing what we are doing, we're here for the common good, and stay busy.
- Get chairs from area and put in the rooms, esp chairs in the waiting room (corner room).
- Facilitate an organized and timely movement of people, first-come, first-serve.
- Clean up hair, trash, keep area clean.
- In the case of head lice, please notify the parent that we are unable to service them.
- Turn in lists for our records (really just need a count please).
- If time runs out, there will be vouchers to The System for kids haircuts.
- Clean up and put everything back in its place. Rick will be in place to help lead clean-up of this area.

Carnival Team (25-35)
Leaders: Damon, Amanda, Front Parking Lot
Reports to: Rick M: ###-####
Please communicate to your team: why we are doing what we are doing, we're here for the common good, and stay busy.
- Help with groceries after you know your location. Be in place by 8:55am so we can open carnival at 9am.
- Facilitate safe fun at each game and attraction.
- Man at least 2 people per attraction.
- Pick up trash if needed throughout.
- Clean up and put everything back in its place.

Food Area (5-10)
Leaders: Angie, Front Parking Lot
Reports to: Rick M: ###-####
Please communicate to your team: why we are doing what we are doing, we're here for the common good, and stay busy.
- Get tables from back and put in square.
- Set up food.
- Rick & guys from small group are grilling. Angie's team will serve food & drinks to guests & give out water to volunteers.
- Keep food out and a clean area.
- Clean up and put everything back in its place.

Groceries (10-25)
Leaders: Sharon, Exit location
Reports to: Rick M: ###-####
Please communicate to your team: why we are doing what we are doing, we're here for the common good, and stay busy.
- Get tables (Rick will show where they are morning of).
- Head to Convoy truck, follow the supply sheet with what goes in each bag.
- Most likely, we will give 1-2 bags per kid. (Will somewhat depend on day of how many show.) Start with one bag, then we will reevaluate. <u>Give out one bag per grocery pass.</u>
- Offer to carry groceries to guest's car.
- Clean up and put everything back in its place (tables go in kitchen).

Photography – Nate   Videography – Michael
Helocopter – Joshua   Fire Truck – Willard Fire Department

Event Invitation to Kids K-5th Grade (sent 8 weeks prior to the event).

Reminder to Kids K-5th Grade that have signed up for event (sent 1 week prior to event).

Floor Plan for Day of Event (this is for set up and leader use).

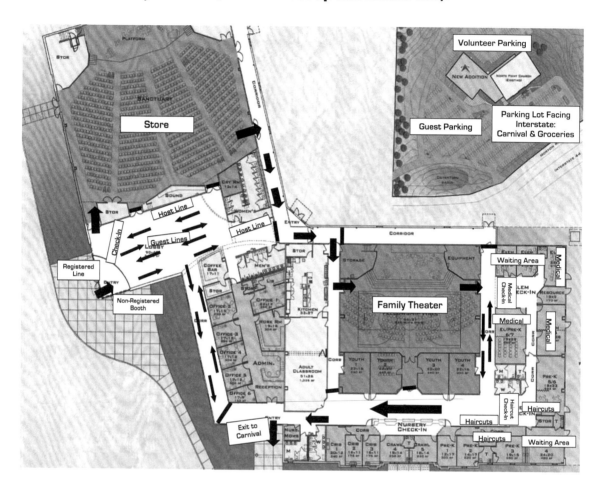

Guest Card (used for information to the guest).

FREQUENTLY ASKED QUESTIONS

WHAT IS NPC'S BACK 2 SCHOOL BASH?
It's just as it sounds; North Point Church wanted to provide an unforgettable Back 2 School Bash to families of K-5 students. Everything is free, no strings attached! The only requirement was registration and that you brought your K-5 student(s). For those who registered and showed up today at 9am with your K-5 student(s), we want to provide your student(s) with free shoes, socks, underwear and a toy plus a bag of groceries, a carnival & lunch, sports/school physicals and haircuts - all free!

WHAT IF I DIDN'T REGISTER FOR TODAY'S GIVEAWAY?
We are glad you are here! If you did not register but showed up today at 9am with your K-5 student(s), you'll still have free access to the carnival & lunch which opens at 9am. There may be the possibility to receive free groceries and some of the free items. If any items are available, you will be called from the carnival area by the number on your ZONE PASS.

HOW DO I REGISTER FOR FUTURE NPC EVENTS?
As instructed on all of our mailers, families with K-5 students called NPC in mid-June/July to register. We communicate future giveaway events through schools and other local organizations.

DO I NEED TO HANG ONTO THIS CARD?
No, but you do need to hang on to the ZONE PASS you received and the GROCERY PASS if you received one.

WHAT IF MY K-5 STUDENT(S) AREN'T WITH ME TODAY?
We are sorry, but this event was specifically designed for families of K-5 students – Your K-5 student(s) need to be with you today to take part.

DO YOU WANT MY FAMILY TO STAY TOGETHER TODAY?
Yes, as much as possible we would like families to stay together. If you were to become accidently separated from your family, we'll direct everyone to the grill area as a central meeting place.

Grocery Pass (given to guests to receive groceries before they leave event).

Host Checklist (used to help those that are hosting guests through facilities so they don't forget important instructions; also to provide helpful things to talk about).

host checklist

Enjoy yourself! Make small talk about school, summer, etc. Care about the family you are hosting. Tell them what we are offering today (info below). And most important: HAVE FUN!

Go Through The Store

-At the store, each registered kid (k-5th grade) will receive play money for them to exchange for a pair of new shoes, underwear, socks & a toy.

-They will go through and pick out what they would like themselves.

-Encourage them and just have fun helping them shop!

Family Theater

-We are offering a theater show in the Children's Auditorium for families to see - there will be games and giveaways!

-Family Theater is a place where kids bring their parents to learn. We offer it on a weekly basis at NPC. Kids learn about virtues such as patience, wisdom, kindness, peace, and hope.

Physicals & Haircuts

-We are offering free school/sports physicals for the kids. There are other medical services offered like dental check-ups and basic check-ups. We are also offering free haircuts to the students.

This is where the host & guest family separates.

-If the guest family stops to get a physical.

-If they stop to get a haircut.

-If they do not want/need either of these services, walk them to the doors that lead out to the carnival.

Thank them for coming and then go back in line to host another family.

Enjoy Carnival

-The carnival is free for you to take your kids and have fun. There will be a fire truck & helicopter too! Plus free lunch - hot dogs, cookies, chips & drinks.

Groceries on Way Out

-Before they leave, they should stop over by the grocery area to exchange thier grocery ticket with a bag of groceries.

Zone Pass (used for those that did not register for event but hope to receive part of the giveaways).

Example 2: Work Project at Convoy of Hope

Rally Notes

Bullet Points For Rally at church campus:

- Welcome --- Are you ready to make an ImpACT?!?! (Applause)
- This is exciting --- Two campuses, one bigger ImpACT
- I know we have some new people to ImpACT --- Who's first ImpACT 2nd Saturday event is this?! (Applause)
- We are going to Convoy of Hope in a few minutes where we'll give you more direction on what we are doing today
- As we explained in the email to you this week, we will be bused over to Convoy and we need everyone to ride the bus
- We give some important direction on the bus and we have an agreement with Convoy that volunteers won't be driving
- We promise to have you back here by 12pm or sooner
- Receiving those emails about this important info is a perk of registering… And registering for this event really helps us plan – so thank you!
- Let's go get on the buses!!!

Adam at Convoy (2 min):

- Welcome North Point Church!
- This is a special month – this is the first time in NPC history that we have two campuses at an ImpACT event (applause)
- We are partnering with Convoy of Hope and Feed My Starving Children today
- We are going to get more direction here in a moment
- Last year some of you may remember we did this project… Then just a couple weeks later the earthquake in Haiti hit.
- One of the countries that Feed My Starving Children focuses it's support on it Haiti.
- Sometimes we meet needs and when we make ourselves available to God, he can put opportunities in front of us before we even realize it
- Something else that will happen here today that is important is that you will get to meet new people
- One of the best ways to get to know people at NPC is through serving
- It's for that reason I want to let the NPC Connections team say hi to you

Tim/Danny (Connections Team) at Convoy (2 min):

- Introduce yourself
- I love these ImpACT events and Adam is right, they are a great way to get to know people
- Tell them you and your team is available on the weekends and you want to help them get connected
- Fellowship is so important and Pastor Tommy has spent this last series talking about how important relationships are
- No pressure today, have fun, get to know people… If you want to start a group with someone you meet today find me by the Connections Center this weekend
- Let's pray

Leader Notes

LEADER INSTRUCTIONS
Second Saturday ● Convoy of Hope ● February 12, 2011

Overview
We are partnering with Convoy of Hope and Feed My Starving Children to pack 75,000 meals in 2+ hours for starving children in other countries!

Day Of Plan

8:00	Rally for volunteers led by Adam at Norton Rd campus "NRC"
	Rally lead by Troy at E. Sunshine campus "ESC"
8:15	Load buses and leave for COH
8:30	Volunteers arrive, unload and gather
8:35	Welcome & brief orientation
8:50	Training
9:00	Allocate volunteers to packing cells and begin
9:00-11:15	Mobile Meal-Packing Party
11:15	Brief clean-up, volunteers load buses
11:30	Buses depart to return to both campuses.

Packing Cells Leaders:

Packing Cells 1&2:	Rich & Janet	Packing Cells 9&10:	Sonny & Sara
Packing Cells 3&4:	Richard & Margaret	Packing Cells 11&12:	Walt & Kristen
Packing Cells 5&6:	Dustin & Jess	Packing Cells 13&14:	Justin & Chad
Packing Cells 7&8:	Charlie & Sarah	Packing Cells 15&16:	Craig & Grant

Drive and meet Jamie at 7:45 am at Convoy of Hope at 330 S. Patterson Ave. (off of E. Chestnut Exp.). Park in striped parking spaces along either the south or west fence lines. Enter through the blue door under the "Logistics" sign.
There are 16 packing cell areas, each with 15 volunteer spots. Leaders will help oversee the production flow of the volunteers working in the 16 packing cell areas *with the instruction you'll see during orientation.* Help people connect with others *and* celebrate changed lives that will happen as a result of this effort.

Greeters – NRC= Alysia & Curtis; ESC= Julie, Gina
Arrive at your respective campus at 7:30am to greet the Second Saturday volunteers at the doors.

Café – NRC= Jennifer; ESC= Sherry
Arrive at your respective campus at 7:30am to serve coffee for the Second Saturday volunteers.

Bus Leaders – NRC= Julie, Clarissa, Cambria, Damon
ESC= Jada & Tyler, Amanda, Charlie
Arrive at your respective campus at 7:30 am at the Café area (NRC meet Kelly Dudley; ESC meet Scott McDonald) for instruction.

Photographer/Videographer – Adie & Andy

Nurse - Jaime M: ###-#### (bringing own vehicle and first aid kit)

Clothing - Wear comfortable shoes for standing and work clothes (layers, it will be cool in the warehouse). Most volunteers will be standing the whole time. There may be some seat-positions for those who need it.

Name tags - Labels for name tags for volunteers will be distributed on the bus to facilitate en route. It will help people co0nnect and learn each other's names. We'll have name tags available for the leaders that arrive by car.

Waiver Form – A waiver of liability should be completed by each individual on the bus en route, and turned in at COH. We'll have waivers available for the site leaders to sign.

Age restriction – Children age 10 and older are welcome to attend and participate.

Coats – Place on tables inside entrance

Restrooms - You'll be shown where the restrooms are upon arrival. Several at the front near the entrance.

CONTACT NUMBERS

Lisa – ###-####	Jamie – ###-####	Randy (COH) – ###-####
Adam – ###-####	Jeff (COH) – ###-####	Lisa (COH) – ###-####
Kelly – ###-####	Scott – ###-####	

Bus Leader Notes

Bus Driver Name:_____

Bus Leader "TO EVENT" Instructions

- Take bus number sign out of your bag & put in the window.
- Load people on bus and take a head count. _____ Make sure people know what bus number they are on.
- Have volunteers put on nametags.
- Pass out waivers and have them signed.
- Give overview of event to participants as you travel to event.
- Once on site, collect waivers as people get off bus. Remind people to get on same bus on the way back. Head into Convoy of Hope. Give waivers to Jamie Swenka when get there.
- **INSTRUCT THE BUS DRIVERS to be back in place at Convoy of Hope for departure at 10:45am in the event we complete the project early.**

Event Overview: Read to Participants on way to Event

Today we will be heading to Convoy of Hope, a local non-profit organization that helps fight NPC's ImpACT initiative of the 4 global giants: Poverty, Disease, Spiritual Emptiness & Illiteracy.

The mission of Convoy of Hope is being a faith-based organization with a driving passion to feed the world through children's feeding initiatives, community outreaches, disaster response, and partner resourcing.

This month, Convoy of Hope & North Point Church along with other people in the community, are working with Feed My Starving Children, another non-profit that's mission is to feed God's starving children hungry in body & spirit.

We are having a MobilePacking Event! At this event today, NPC will pack over 75,000 meals to feed children all over the world. How exciting to think about!

We will be meeting up with the other North Point Church Campus – all working together to make one GIANT IMPACT!

Bus Leader "FROM EVENT" Instructions

- Load people on bus and take a head count: _____ (make sure it matches previous #)
- Take bus # sign out of window and put in your bag.
- Give overview of event to participants as you travel from event.
- Once back at church, dismiss vols to cars for everyone to leave. Church will not be open for use.
- **RETURN THE BUS LEADER TOTE BAG WITH EVERYTHING IN IT TO YOUR LEADER**

Event Overview: Read to Participants on way from Event

Thank you for serving today. With your generosity and kindness, you have made an IMPACT nationally and worldwide through partnership with Convoy of Hope. We were able to attack the pillars of POVERTY, DISEASE and SPIRITUAL EMPTINESS.

If you want more information about Convoy or how to partner with them individually, you can go to their website at convoyofhope.org. Also, every Tuesday night from 6:30 – 8:30pm is "Hands of Hope" a volunteer project that does many of the things we did today. No registration is necessary.

Again, a big thank you. Don't forget to sign up for the 2nd Saturday in March!

When we arrive at the church, it will be closed, so you can hop in your car and enjoy the rest of the day.

See you tonight or tomorrow at Church for another unforgettable experience!

FUND-RAISING TIPS

Professional fund-raising groups will tell you that to raise the most money or to get the most involvement in a "cause" you need the 2 "I's":

(1) INFORM people at the highest level;

(2) INVOLVE people at the highest level.

If you answer all questions people may have and give them a role in the initiative, they will want to contribute at a high level. Then you recruit them to recruit others (use their influence) to join in. That's when people really have a stake in the project.

Here are a few practical ways people can come up with money to give:

- Give cash;

- Sell a car, and give the money;

- Sell a second home, and donate the proceeds;

- Get a second job so as to have additional income to give;

- Eliminate extras like cable TV, Starbucks, lunch out, movies, etc.;

- Car pool to conserve gas money, and donate the savings;

- Delay major purchases in order to give money instead.

IMPACT FAQS

- **How do I get enough volunteers?**

  - Promote! Talk about it on stage, in the weekly bulletin, online, through your news program, through mailers. This is to start off. At some point (you decide), you will not have to promote as heavily due to word of mouth. Word of mouth is always the most effective. It really helps for the lead pastor/speaker to talk about ImpACT on stage.

- **How do I find potential partners?**

  - Research your community. Check out the organizations that are already helping. Talk to them, and let them know what you are doing. Let them know there are no strings attached. Research online, find partners in the phone book, use your contacts in the community, etc. The hardest part will probably be letting them know NO STRINGS ATTACHED. Many places might be hesitant until they see that you really mean no strings attached.

- **How am I going to find time to do these events?**

  - Hire the right people. You don't have to be at all of the events. An appearance is nice, but hire someone (it could be a volunteer position) that knows how to talk to other organizations and can plan an event well. You don't have to do everything! And remember the Chapter 10 margin principle.

- **My church attendance is 400 people. How many volunteers will I have?**

  - It's up to you. About 7 to 10 percent of NPC's attendees participate in any given event.

- **What if not all the volunteers that signed up, show up?**

  - Always plan with margin in mind. We can normally expect 70-80 percent to show up. We have had turnouts of 50 percent, and we still complete the projects. When talking to ImpACT partners, always give them a range for the project.

- **We didn't finish the project. What should we do?**

  - Always finish! If you don't, they may not want to work with you again. Even if after the event you have to go in and clean up, do it! Make sure the experience your partner organization has with your church is an amazing one – before, during and after the event.

- **What if my first project fails?**

  - Try again. Plan better. Make sure you have the right people in place. Make the best of it.

- **I have too many volunteers for our next project. What should I do?**

  ○ Come up with another project. There might be something you can add at the organization you are partnering with or you can find something at your church. Do a deep clean, and let them know it is for changed lives! Do something that you don't have the manpower to do on staff but that you have been wanting to do. Find another organization that could use help.

2ND SATURDAY FOR SMALLER CHURCH/ LARGER CHURCH

Smaller Church	Larger Church
Partner with another church to add more volunteers if partnering with a larger organization	Utilize your current volunteers within the church while partnering with a larger organization
Help a smaller organization that a larger church couldn't help	Help a larger organization that a smaller church or group couldn't help
Tell your story to the media	Tell your story to the media
Go out into the field with a smaller group to make a large impact	Stay to replenish the needs of the organization that is sending small teams out into the field
Organize donations	Bring in donations
Focus on the few things that are important to you at your church and say no to the rest	Focus on the things that are important to you at your church and say no to the rest
Do projects based on specialized volunteers	Do projects anyone at any skill set can do
Utilize a volunteer staff role for positions referenced in Chapter 7	Hire staff to fill the key leadership roles referenced in Chapter 7
Do less projects a year and ask for a higher participation level out of your church	Do 8-12 projects a year and expect at least 10% participation of your total attendees
Encourage 100% participation	Encourage 100% participation